Reproduction, storage, adaptation or translation, in any form or by any means, of this public
written permission of the publisher. Excerpts may be reproduced for the purpose of research,
by educational institutions solely for educational purposes, without permission, providing

C000295699

First Published in the UK in 2014 by Focus Education (UK) Ltc
Updated August 2015
Reprinted September 2015
Updated January 2018
Updated October 2018
Updated October 2019

Focus Education (UK) Ltd
Talking Point Conference and Exhibition Centre
Huddersfield Road
Scouthead
Saddleworth
OL4 4AG

Focus Education (UK) Ltd Reg. No 4507968
ISBN 978-1-909038-28-8

Companies, institutions and other organisations wishing to make bulk purchases of books published by
Focus Education should contact their local bookstore or Focus Education direct:

Customer Services, Focus Education, Talking Point Conference and Exhibition Centre,
Huddersfield Road, Scouthead, Saddleworth, OL4 4AG
Tel 01457 821818 Fax 01457 878205

www.focus-education.co.uk
customerservice@focus-education.co.uk
Printed in Great Britain by Focus Education UK Ltd, Scouthead

Users should be fully aware that the government may change any element of their descriptors and guidance.
This document was wholly accurate at the date of publication.

Introduction

- The purpose of this publication is to help schools and academies to track the progress made by pupils on a term by term basis (core subjects) and on an annual basis for non core subjects and science. The information should guide teachers to make judgements as to whether individuals are on track or not to meet the national standards for their year group by the end of the year.
- **For non-core subjects and also for science** there is greater account given to the 'knowledge' that pupils should have acquired. This is to be in line with the greater focus on the 'substance of education'.
- We are therefore assuming that the wealth of human knowledge that we choose to pass on to our learners should be at the heart of education.
- Apart from science, the National Curriculum sets out its programmes of study in key stages. Therefore many assumptions have been made about when to cover certain elements of the programme.
- It may be that your school may need to consider when certain aspects are being taught and make modifications to the key assessment criteria accordingly.

Introduction (continued)

Reading

- The reading section effectively, in the first instance, takes account of pupils' ability at Key Stage 1 to decode words and apply their phonic knowledge. Later this checks their ability to skim read and read common exception words, noting the unusual correspondences between spelling and sound. There is also a section relating to pupils' comprehension skills, which are broken into reading for pleasure and reading for accuracy, fluency and understanding at Key Stage 1.
- At Key Stage 2, there are statements directly related to maintaining a positive attitude to reading as well as justifying their views.

Writing

- The writing section looks at pupils' ability to deal with spelling, punctuation and handwriting (transcriptional skills) and compositional skills. The compositional skills include grammatical features and structure. As is anticipated, there is a clear link between reading and writing.

Mathematics

- Although there is a suggested progression on a term by term basis the statements may need to be moved slightly between terms to take full account of what has been taught each term. Not surprisingly, number features highly as do the four calculation operations. Measurement and geometry pay an important part with algebra, and ratio and proportion being a feature in Year 6.

Key Assessment Criteria
Reading

Year 1

Aspect	Autumn	Spring	Summer
Applying Phonics	• I know when to use phonic knowledge to decode words. • I read common words using phonic knowledge, where possible. • I read words of more than one syllable that contain taught GPCs. • I read phonically decodable texts.	• I know which parts of words can be decoded using phonics. • I blend sounds in unfamiliar words based on known GPCs. • I read words with familiar endings - s, es, ing, ed, er, est. • I read words which have the prefix –un added. • I read phonically decodable texts, with confidence. • I divide words into syllables, for example, pocket, rabbit, carrot, thunder, sunset.	• I hear and recognise all 40+ phonemes. • I match all 40+ graphemes to their phonemes (Phase 3). • I identify all 40+ graphemes in my reading. • I know that words can have omitted letters and that an apostrophe represents the omitted letters. • I find contractions in my reading. • I read words with contractions. • I read compound words, for example, football, playground, farmyard, bedroom.
Reading for Pleasure	• I know that there are different kinds of books. • I know the difference between a story book and an information book. • I can find the title, author and the illustrator of a book. • I know some familiar stories. • I recognise familiar story language.	• I say what I like or dislike about a book. • I say if a story reminds me of another story or something that I have experienced. • I listen to others' ideas about a book. • I find familiar story language in stories read aloud to me or ones I have read independently. • I retell key stories orally using narrative language. • I recognise rhyming language.	• I say whether I agree or disagree with other's ideas. • I say whether I agree or disagree with others' ideas. • I say why I agree or disagree with ideas. • I recognise repeated or patterned language. • I recognise patterned language in the poems and rhymes I know. • I know some poems and rhymes by heart.

Year 1 (continued)

Aspect	Autumn	Spring	Summer
Reading Accurately, with Fluency and with Understanding	• I use picture clues to support my understanding. • I use picture cues to deepen my understanding. • I identify the characters in a story. • I recognise a character's feelings. • I say why a character has a feeling.	• I use prior knowledge to understand texts. • I identify unfamiliar words and ask about meaning. • I use the context to make informed guesses about the meaning of unfamiliar words. • I make predictions based on the events in the story. • I give an opinion about a character. • I know that stories can have similar characters.	• I discuss the meaning of unfamiliar words with others. • I know that stories can have similar patterns of events. • I make links to other stories. • I make links with characters in other stories. • I can answer retrieval questions about a book. • I use information from the story to support my opinion. • I understand that a writer can leave gaps for the reader to fill. • I answer questions which fill the gaps in a story. (Inference)

Year 2

Aspect	Autumn	Spring	Summer
Applying Phonics	▪ I understand the importance of decoding words automatically. ▪ I understand that some words cannot be decoded with phonic strategies. ▪ I use the graphemes taught to blend sounds. ▪ I know that phonemes may be represented by different graphemes. ▪ I know that familiar words do not need to be sounded out and blended. ▪ I read these familiar words automatically and accurately without sounding or blending.	▪ I know that the same grapheme may be read in different ways. ▪ I recognise alternatives and consider which will make more sense. ▪ I recognise syllables in words. ▪ I know that breaking words into syllables helps fluent decoding. ▪ I know that other strategies can be used to read unfamiliar words. ▪ I use other strategies to support fluent decoding.	▪ I read words of two or more syllables accurately. ▪ I read aloud books closely matched to my improving phonic knowledge, sounding out unfamiliar words accurately, automatically and without undue hesitation. ▪ I read these books fluently and confidently.
Reading for Pleasure	▪ I know that there are different kinds of stories. ▪ I listen to or read a range of different kinds of stories. ▪ I make choices about the books I read. ▪ I know that non-fiction books are organised differently from fiction texts. ▪ I know that books or texts have a purpose.	▪ I explain why I prefer certain books or stories. ▪ I can retell stories with the key events in the correct sequence. ▪ I can retell a story with the key events and the characters. ▪ I know how to find information in a non-fiction book. ▪ I identify the purpose of a book or a text. ▪ I know that books and stories are set in different places and times.	▪ I decide how useful a non-fiction book is to find the information I need. ▪ I can find the setting or time in books or stories. ▪ I can discuss the setting or time in books.

Year 2 (continued)

Aspect	Autumn	Spring	Summer
Reading for Pleasure – Poetry	▪ I know the difference between poetry and narrative ▪ I know that there are different kinds of poetry. ▪ I listen to different kinds of poetry. ▪ I talk about books or poems read. ▪ I know that stories and poems can have patterned or recurring literary language.	▪ I talk about the meaning of different poems. ▪ I recognise that a poem can tell a story. ▪ I learn a poem by heart. ▪ I give an opinion on books or poems read. ▪ I find patterned or recurring literary language in poems and stories. ▪ I find favourite words and phrases.	▪ I recite or perform a poem making the meaning clear. ▪ I talk about favourite words and phrases. ▪ I know that word choice affects meaning. ▪ I can explain why a writer has chosen a word to affect meaning.
Reading Accurately, with Fluency and with Understanding	▪ I know that the purpose of reading is to make meaning. ▪ I know that there is a range of decoding strategies. ▪ I check that text I read makes sense. ▪ I re-read when I have lost the meaning.	▪ I self-correct when I have lost the meaning. ▪ I use prior knowledge and reading experiences to understand text. ▪ I use the context to understand texts. ▪ I ask questions to clarify understanding. ▪ I can find the answers to retrieval questions about stories, poems or non-fiction texts. ▪ I recognise that a writer can have a message for the reader. ▪ I can make predictions about possible events.	▪ I know what the inference - 'reading between the lines'- means. ▪ I find inferences about characters' feelings and thoughts. ▪ I can explain inferences about characters' feelings and thoughts. ▪ I give reasons for characters' actions or behaviour. ▪ I recognise key ideas in a text. ▪ I can explain a writer's message. ▪ I can make predictions about how characters might behave.

Year 3

Aspect	Autumn	Spring	Summer
Applying Phonics	• I know that phonics is one strategy to help me read unfamiliar words. • I know when phonic strategies will help me to read a word and when they will not. • I know what a root word is. • I understand how to use a root word to help me read unfamiliar words. • I use root words to help me read unfamiliar words. • I use root words to help me understand the meaning of unfamiliar words. • I know what prefixes and suffixes are. • I understand how prefixes and suffixes can change the meaning of a word. • I prefixes and suffixes to read unfamiliar words. • I prefixes and suffixes to understand the meaning of unfamiliar words.	• I apply knowledge of root words, prefixes and suffixes to read aloud and to understand the meaning of unfamiliar words. • I know that some words may have a similar pronunciation but may be written differently. • I know that some of these are unusual. • I use knowledge of unusual phoneme/grapheme correspondences to help me read unfamiliar words. • I know that unfamiliar words can be read by using knowledge of similar words (analogy).	• I use analogy, drawing on the pronunciation of similar known words to read others.

Year 3 (continued)

Aspect	Autumn	Spring	Summer
Reading for Pleasure	<ul><li>I know that there are different kinds of narrative stories.</li><li>I understand that a sequence of events in a narrative is called the plot.</li><li>I can identify the plot in a narrative.</li><li>I use a dictionary to check or find the meaning of new words.</li><li>I know that there are different kinds of non-fiction books.</li><li>I know that non-fiction books are structured in different ways.</li><li>I know how to use a non-fiction book to find identified information.</li><li>I identify any words that are unfamiliar.</li></ul>	<ul><li>I understand that narratives can have differently structured plots.</li><li>I talk about the different plot structures in genres read.</li><li>I know that writers choose words and language to create an effect on the reader.</li><li>I find effective words and language in reading that writers have used to create effects.</li><li>I discuss a range of narrative stories and their similarities and differences.</li><li>I choose books for specific purposes.</li><li>I discuss the meaning of unfamiliar words identified.</li></ul>	<ul><li>I recognise the literary language typical of narrative genres read.</li><li>I recognise words and language that show the setting of a book – historical, cultural or social.</li><li>I explain why a writer makes choices about words and language used.</li><li>I discuss meaning of specific or unusual words used by authors to create effects.</li><li>I explain why a writer has chosen specific words and language.</li><li>I record words and language from reading to use in my own writing.</li><li>I make connections between books written by the same author.</li><li>I re-tell some of stories written by the same author by heart.</li></ul>

Year 3 (continued)

Aspect	Autumn	Spring	Summer
Reading for Pleasure - Poetry	▪ I know that there are different forms of poetry. ▪ I recognise and name different types of poems which have been introduced. ▪ I know that words and language in poems create effects.	▪ I can discuss the meaning of words and language in poems. ▪ I understand that there can be more than one interpretation of a poem. ▪ I understand that the meaning of poems can be enhanced through performance. ▪ I watch performances of poems.	▪ I discuss how the meaning is enhanced through performance. ▪ I identify that intonation, tone, volume and action can be used to enhance meaning. ▪ I prepare poems to read aloud and to perform, showing understanding through intonation, tone, volume and action.
Reading Accurately, with Fluency and with Understanding	▪ II check understanding in any book or text that I read. ▪ I ask questions to ensure understanding of a text. ▪ I know that there will be unfamiliar words in a text. ▪ I know that texts have a main idea. ▪ I identify the main idea of a text. ▪ I know that the organisation and layout of a book helps me to understand it. ▪ I know how to find key words or information in a non-fiction text.	▪ I ask questions to deepen understanding of a text. ▪ I use the context of unfamiliar words to explain their meaning. ▪ I give a personal response to a text. ▪ I use evidence from the text to support my response. ▪ I use clues from the text to predict what might happen next. ▪ I know that the main idea in a narrative may also have a message for the reader. ▪ I know that the message in a book is called the theme. ▪ I recognise that books may have similar themes. ▪ I understand that the organisation and layout may be different according to the purpose of the book. ▪ I record key words or information found in a non-fiction text.	▪ I check the meaning of any unfamiliar words through questioning, discussion or use of dictionaries. ▪ I explain my personal response. ▪ I listen to others' personal responses to a text. ▪ I adapt own response in the light of others' responses. ▪ I know that characters' actions can tell the reader about their thoughts, feelings and motives. ▪ I infer characters' feelings, thoughts and motives from their actions. ▪ I give reasons for predicting what might happen next. ▪ I identify the organisation and layout in books. ▪ I explain how the organisation and layout helps me to understand it.

Year 4

Aspect	Autumn	Spring	Summer
Applying Phonics	<ul><li>I know that phonics is one strategy to read unfamiliar words.</li><li>I know when phonic strategies will help to read a word and when they will not.</li><li>I use knowledge of root words to help me read unfamiliar words.</li><li>I use root words to help me understand the meaning of unfamiliar words.</li><li>I use knowledge of learned prefixes and suffixes to help me read unfamiliar words.</li><li>I use prefixes and suffixes to help me understand the meaning of unfamiliar words.</li></ul>	<ul><li>I apply knowledge of root words, prefixes and suffixes to help me read aloud and to understand the meaning of unfamiliar words.</li><li>I know that many words may have a similar pronunciation but may be written differently.</li><li>I know that some of these are unusual.</li><li>I use knowledge of unusual phoneme/grapheme correspondences to help me read unfamiliar words.</li><li>I know that unfamiliar words can be read by using knowledge of known similar words (analogy).</li><li>I use analogy drawing on the pronunciation of similar known words to read others</li></ul>	
Reading for Pleasure	<ul><li>I know that there is a range of narrative stories.</li><li>I discuss the range of narrative stories introduced so far and consider differences and similarities.</li><li>I understand that these have different plot patterns.</li><li>I know that the plot develops in different ways according to the plot pattern.</li><li>I use a dictionary to check or find the meaning of new words.</li><li>I find similarities in the books I read.</li><li>I understand that writers open stories in different ways.</li></ul>	<ul><li>I understand that a writer can use patterned language for effect.</li><li>I find examples of patterned language for effect.</li><li>I identify words and language that show the setting of a book – historical, cultural or social.</li><li>I know that writers choose words and language to show atmosphere, mood or feelings.</li><li>I find words and language in my reading that writers have used to show atmosphere, mood or feelings.</li><li>I identify different openings in different books and I can compare different story openings.</li></ul>	<ul><li>I explain how the writer has used words and language to show the setting of a book.</li><li>I explain how the words and language used show atmosphere, mood or feelings.</li><li>I explain why a writer has chosen specific words and language to create mood, atmosphere or feelings.</li><li>I record words and language from my reading to use in my own writing.</li><li>I find similarities in the use of language and openings in books experienced.</li></ul>

Year 4 (continued)

Aspect	Autumn	Spring	Summer
Reading for Pleasure - Poetry	▪ I know that there are different forms of poetry. ▪ I know that *words* and language in poems create effects.	▪ I recognise and name different types of poems which have been introduced to me. ▪ I explain the effect created by the poet's choice of words and language. ▪ I know that poems may have patterned language. ▪ I find examples of patterned language in the poems I read. ▪ I explain the effect of patterned language in poems and why a poet might use it. ▪ I understand that the meaning of poems can be enhanced through performance. ▪ I enjoy watching performances of poems.	▪ I discuss how the meaning of a poem is enhanced through performance. ▪ I identify that intonation, tone, volume and action can be used to enhance meaning. ▪ I prepare poems to read aloud and to perform, showing understanding through intonation, tone, volume and action.
Reading for Pleasure – Non-Fiction	▪ I choose a specific non-fiction book for a specific purpose. ▪ I identify any words that are unfamiliar to me. ▪ I use dictionaries to check or find the meaning of unfamiliar words.	▪ I know where to find the specific information needed in my book. ▪ I know how to use a non-fiction book to find identified information. ▪ I discuss the meaning of the unfamiliar words identified.	

Year 4 (continued)

Aspect	Autumn	Spring	Summer
Reading with understanding	• I frequently empathise with a character. • I identify the main idea/s of a text. • I know that the main idea of a text can be summarised in a sentence. • I know that many books have themes. • I discuss the possible theme/s in books. • I identify a theme in a book. • I know that the organisation and layout of books vary according to the purpose of the book.	• I understand that a reader needs to interact with a text to understand it fully. • I check understanding in any book or text read. • I actively seek the meaning of any words or language not understood. • I ask questions to ensure understanding of a text. • I check the meaning of any unfamiliar words through questioning, discussion or use of dictionaries. • I understand that a writer wants the reader to respond in a certain way. • I explain how the writer made sure of the reader's response, using evidence from the text. • I compare with others' personal responses to a text. • I understand why a character acted, responded or felt in a certain way. • I make predictions based on the text and from knowledge from other books. • I identify the main idea in paragraphs in a text. • I summarise the main idea of a text in a sentence. • I find evidence which shows what the theme is in a book. • I explain why the evidence shows what the theme is. • I use the organisation and layout of a book to find specific information. • I record key words or information found	• I ask questions to deepen understanding of a text – between and beyond the lines. • I find where the writer has written to make the reader respond in a certain way. • I adapt my own response in the light of others' responses. • I understand why a writer wanted the character to respond in a certain way. • I infer meaning using evidence from events, description and dialogue. • I make connections with books with similar themes. • I skim to find specific information on a page or in a paragraph. • I scan a page or paragraph to find key words or information.

Year 5

Aspect	Autumn	Spring	Summer
Applying Phonics	• I apply knowledge of root words, prefixes and suffixes to read aloud and to understand the meaning of unfamiliar words. • I read further exception words, noting the unusual correspondences between spelling and sound, and where these occur in the word. • I attempt pronunciation of unfamiliar words drawing on prior knowledge of similar looking words.		
Reading for Pleasure – maintaining a positive attitude about reading	• I know that there is a range of narrative genres which includes classic and traditional stories, myths and legends, poems and play scripts. • I know that these are structured in different ways. • I know that non-fiction texts are structured to guide the reader to information. • I can explain how the structure guides the reader to find specific information. • I find words and language that are used for effect. • I can explain how the words and language create a precise effect.	• I discuss and explain how and why different books have different structures. • I can explain why I enjoyed a book or poem and who might also enjoy it. • I evaluate the usefulness of a non-fiction book to research questions raised. • I understand that a writer moves events forward through a balance of dialogue, action and description. • I record effective words and language from reading to use in my own writing.	• I can explore how dialogue is used to develop character. • I can explore how actions are added to dialogue to move events forward. • I understand that writers use language for precise effect. • I understand that this may include precise nouns, precisely chosen adjectives, well developed noun phrases, similes, metaphors, personification etc. • I understand that a writer uses different sentence structures and techniques to create effects. • I can explore the structures and techniques used. For example, short sentences, rhetorical questions, ellipsis, flashbacks. • I can record examples of effective techniques and structures from reading to use in my writing.

Year 5 (continued)

Aspect	Autumn	Spring	Summer
Reading for Pleasure - comprehension	▪ I understand that there will be unfamiliar words in the texts I read. ▪ I use dictionaries to check or find the meaning of unfamiliar words. ▪ I ask questions to improve my understanding. ▪ I re-read to check that the text is meaningful. ▪ I draw inferences such as inferring characters' feelings, thoughts and motives from their actions at different points in the text.	▪ I use meaning-seeking strategies to explore the meaning of words in context. ▪ I understand that inferences can be drawn from different parts of the text. ▪ I justify inferences with evidence from the text. ▪ I make predictions from evidence found and implied. ▪ I summarise the main ideas drawn from a text.	▪ I use meaning – seeking strategies to explore the meaning of idiomatic and figurative language. ▪ I understand that inferences can be made by reading between and beyond the lines. ▪ I know that the context in which it was written can affect a text. For example, a classic text reflects how an audience of that time will react. ▪ I explain how the context of a text reflects the reaction of the audience it was written for.
Reading for Pleasure – justifications for views	▪ I give a personal point of view about a text. ▪ I explain the reasons for my viewpoint, using evidence from the text. ▪ I listen to others' ideas and opinions about a text. ▪ I make connections between other similar texts, prior knowledge and experience. ▪ I explain why there are connections, using evidence. ▪ I compare books with similar themes.	▪ I build on others' ideas and opinions about a text in discussion. ▪ I question others' ideas about a text. ▪ I compare different versions of texts. ▪ I explain the similarities and differences between different versions of texts. ▪ I explain how books written in different contexts can have similar themes.	▪ I evaluate the effectiveness of different versions of texts.

Year 5 (continued)

Aspect	Autumn	Spring	Summer
Retrieving Information from Text	▪ I identify key information from my text. ▪ I summarise key information in sentences. ▪ I find key information from different parts of the text. ▪ I understand the difference between fact and opinion. ▪ I find examples of fact and opinion in texts and explain why one is fact and the other opinion.	▪ I use skimming and scanning to find the information I need. ▪ I make notes on the information I need. ▪ I organise my notes and present information. ▪ I summarise key information from different parts of the text. ▪ I present an oral overview or summary of a text. ▪ I understand that a narrative can be told from different points of view – narrator, character. ▪ I identify the point of view in a narrative. ▪ I understand that the writer may have a viewpoint.	▪ I explore how events are viewed from another perspective. ▪ I explain the writer's viewpoint with evidence from the text. ▪ I identify the writer's viewpoint, for example, how different characters are presented.

Year 6

Aspect	Autumn	Spring	Summer
Applying Phonics	<ul><li>I apply knowledge of root words, prefixes and suffixes to read aloud and to understand the meaning of unfamiliar words.</li><li>I read further exception words, noting the unusual correspondences between spelling and sound, and where these occur in the word.</li><li>I attempt pronunciation of unfamiliar words drawing on prior knowledge of similar looking words.</li></ul>		
Reading for Pleasure – Maintaining a positive attitude about reading	<ul><li>I am familiar with a range of narrative genres which includes classic and traditional stories, myths and legends, poems and play scripts.</li><li>I know that texts can have elements of more than one text type.</li><li>I identify the elements included in a text type.</li><li>I can explain why I enjoyed a book or poem and who might also enjoy it.</li><li>I evaluate the usefulness of a non-fiction book to research questions raised.</li></ul>	<ul><li>I know that non-fiction texts may include a creative, fictional element.</li><li>I can explain how the choices a writer has made about the structure of a text support its purpose.</li><li>I can make predictions using knowledge of the conventions of different genres and text types.</li><li>I understand that non-fiction texts may present the same information with different viewpoints.</li><li>I identify the characteristics of a writer's style.</li><li>I know that the word and language choices support the writer's purpose.</li><li>I can record examples of words and language from reading to use in my own writing.</li></ul>	<ul><li>I know that style and vocabulary are linked to the purpose of the text.</li><li>I can explain how the style and vocabulary are linked to the purpose of the text, using evidence.</li><li>I evaluate the usefulness of different non-fiction texts by comparing how different writer's present the same information.</li><li>I can explain the characteristics of a writer's style, using evidence.</li><li>I can explain how the word and language choices support the writer's purpose, using evidence.</li><li>I can explain how the techniques and structures used support the writer's purpose, using evidence.</li><li>I record examples of techniques and structures from reading to use in my own writing.</li><li>I can comment on the effectiveness of the writer's use of language structures and techniques.</li></ul>

Year 6 (continued)

Aspect	Autumn	Spring	Summer
Reading for Pleasure – comprehension	• I understand that there will be unfamiliar words in the texts I read. • I use dictionaries to check or find the meaning of unfamiliar words. • I use meaning-seeking strategies to explore the words in context. • I use meaning – seeking strategies to explore the meaning of idiomatic and figurative language.	• I ask questions to improve and deepen my understanding. • I re-read to check that the text is meaningful. • I know that a text may need to be read slowly or re-read to deepen my understanding. • I know that texts have different layers of meaning – between the lines and beyond the lines. • I summarise the main ideas drawn from a text.	• I can find the different layers of meaning in a text. • I can explain how they contribute to the reader's understanding of the overall meaning, characters, themes. • I make predictions from evidence found and implied. • I know that the context in which it was written can affect a text. For example, a classic text reflects how an audience of that time will react. • I can explain how the context of a text reflects the reaction of the audience it was written for.
Reading for Pleasure – justifications for views	• I give a personal point of view about a text. • I can explain the reasons for a viewpoint, using evidence from the text. • I listen to others' ideas and opinions about a text.	• I build on others' ideas and opinions about a text in discussion. • I question others' ideas about a text. • I make connections between texts which may not initially seem similar. • I can explain why there are connections, using evidence. • I can explain the similarities and differences between different versions of texts.	• I identify themes in books which have different cultural, social or historical contexts. • I compare and contrast themes in a range of books. • I can explain how there are common themes in different books, using evidence from reading.

Year 6 (continued)

Aspect	Autumn	Spring	Summer
Explaining and Discussing own Understanding	▪ I identify key information from a text. ▪ I summarise key information in sentences. ▪ I find key information from different parts of the text. ▪ I summarise key information from different parts of the text. ▪ I present an oral overview or summary of a text. ▪ I understand the difference between fact and opinion. ▪ I find examples of fact and opinion in texts. ▪ I can explain why one example is fact and another is opinion. ▪ I use point, evidence and explanation (PEE) or answer it, prove it, explain it (APE) to respond to questions about texts.	▪ I understand that a narrative can be told from different points of view – narrator, character. ▪ I identify the point of view in a narrative. ▪ I can explore how events are viewed from another perspective. ▪ I identify the techniques used to create feelings, atmosphere, mood or messages. ▪ I can comment on how the writer's intent affects the reader.	▪ I know that points of view can also be implied. ▪ I identify implied points of view. ▪ I can explain implied points of view, using evidence. ▪ I understand that the writer may have a viewpoint. ▪ I identify the writer's viewpoint, for example, how different characters are presented. ▪ I can explain the writer's viewpoint with evidence from the text. ▪ I can explain the effect of the writer's viewpoint on the reader. ▪ I can explain how the techniques used create feelings, atmosphere, mood or messages.

Key Assessment Criteria
Writing

Year 1

Aspect	Autumn	Spring	Summer
Handwriting	• I sit correctly at a table, holding a pencil comfortably and correctly. • I form the digits 0-9 correctly.	• I form lower case letters in the correct direction, starting and finishing in the right place. *(cursive- kicks and flicks)*	• I name the letters of the alphabet in order. • I form capital letters.
Spelling	• I spell unknown words using my phonemes (sounds). *(phonetically plausible attempts: yoo, rayn- rain, sed- said frend for friend)*	• I use the suffixes -ing, -ed, -er and -est where no change is needed in the spelling of root words. • I write from memory simple dictated sentences including the words taught so far.	• I use letter names to show alternative spellings of the same phonemes. • I spell words that use suffixes for plurals or 3rd person. *(E.g.: adding s/es; box, fox, fix, pencil, pen)*
Composition	• I say a sentence out loud before I write it down. *(Hold a sentence)*	• I plan my writing by saying what I am going to write about. *(build a sentence)* • I read my own writing aloud so it can be heard by others and check for sense. *('Oops, I forgot to put a capital letter after that full stop.'; 'I used my sounds to help me spell that long word.')*	• I sequence sentences to form short narratives. *(Beginning/middle/ end- sentences link and build on from each other- The cat walked down the road. It was bright orange and fluffy. It wanted to get home.)* • I use sequence sentences in chronological order to recount an event /experience. *(Basic adverbials for when-First, Then, Next, After that)*
Grammar	• I use the personal pronoun 'I'	• I use 'and' to join ideas within a sentence. *('I went to the park and played on the swing.')*	• I may attempt to use other conjunctions. • I make sure that word choices are relevant to the context and I use word banks to support this. • I begin to use adjectives to add detail to my sentences.
Punctuation	• I leave spaces between words. • I use a capital letter for the start of a sentence.	• I begin to use other punctuation such as exclamation and question marks. • I use a full stop accurately.	• I use capital letters for the names of people, places and days of the week. *(Aa)*

Year 2

Aspect	Autumn	Spring	Summer
Handwriting	• I use some of the diagonal and horizontal strokes needed to join letters. • I understand which letters, when adjacent to one another, are best left unjoined. • I write capital letters (and digits) of the correct size/ orientation to one another.	• I use spacing between words that reflects the size of the letters.	• I form lower case letters of the correct size relative to one another.
Spelling	• I segment spoken words into phonemes and record these as graphemes. *(Single syllable words and multisyllabic words segmented into spoken words and phonemes represented by a phonetically plausible spelling. e.g. yesterday, exsighting, speshal, diffrent)*	• I spell longer words using suffixes such as ment, ness, ful, less, ly *(Root words ending in a consonant- merriment, happiness, plentifull, penniless, happily, quickly, thoughtless/ful/ly)* • I spell common exception words (door, because, sugar, people, - see Year 2 spelling list)	• I use apostrophes for the most common contracted words. *(e.g. don't, won't, I'll, I'm, won't)* • I spell words with different spellings *(multisyllabic words containing new spellings e.g.: race, ice, knock, gnat, typewriter, margarine, muckspreader)* • I identify and apply my knowledge of homophones/ near homophones *(There/their/they're; here/hear; quite/quiet; bare/bear; some/sum; blew/blue; knight/night)*
Composition	• I develop stamina for writing by writing for different purposes. *(Real and fictional/own and other's experiences- including simple narratives, poems and recounts)*	• I plan and discuss the content of my writing. *(Jotting down ideas, planning the structure, oral rehearsal of what they want to say, sentence by sentence)* • I evaluate my writing independently, with peers and with my teacher by making simple additions and corrections. *(Re-reading to check for sense; verbs used correctly E.g. Pupil writes 'I sitted under the tree and eated my lunch' becomes 'sat and ate')* • I write, from memory, simple dictated sentences.	• I proof-read to check for errors in spelling, grammar and punctuation. *(Will spot most of their own spelling and errors quickly. e.g. 'This should be an exclamation because she's shouting for help' 'I forgot to double the p of stop when adding –ing')* • I make changes, sometimes independently and sometimes in discussion with an adult, to improve the effect and impact of my writing.

Year 2 (continued)

Aspect	Autumn	Spring	Summer
Grammar	• My word choices are thoughtful and sometimes ambitious with specific or technical vocabulary used in non-narrative writing.	• I use expanded noun phrases to describe, expand and specify. ('the delicate, blue butterfly flew off into the humid, summer sky') • I use subordination (using when, if, that or because). (Consistent use of both e.g.: You need to pack your raincoat because it is going to rain later.)	• I use sentences with different forms: statements, questions, exclamations and commands. ('The colourful butterfly flew from flower to flower' 'Where do clouds come from?' 'What big eyes you have!' Sift the flour and mix the other ingredients') • I use co-ordination (using or, and or but) You remembered your book bag but forgot your packed lunch.) • I use present and past tenses correctly and consistently including the progressive form. (Consistently makes the correct choice e.g.: 'She is drumming; she drummed, she was drumming' • I use adjectives, adverbs and expanded noun phrases to add detail and specify.
Punctuation	• I use full stops and capital letters- most are correct. (This will be consistent across a range of dictated and independent writing) • I mostly use exclamation and question marks accurately to demarcate sentences.	• I use capital letters for the personal pronoun I and for most proper nouns.	• I begin to use commas to separate items in a list. • I sometimes use apostrophes for singular possession.

Year 3

Aspect	Autumn	Spring	Summer
Handwriting	• I increase the legibility, consistency and quality of my handwriting. • I understand which letters, when adjacent to one another, are best left unjoined. • I use the diagonal and horizontal strokes that are needed to join letters.		
Spelling	• I use the first two or three letters of a word to check its spelling in a dictionary.	• I spell words with additional prefixes and suffixes and understand how to add them to root words. *(from nouns using super, anti, auto)* • I spell correctly word families based on common words. *(solve, solution, solver)* • I identify the root word in longer words.	• I recognise and spell additional homophones. *(he'll/heel/heal)* • I make comparisons from a word already known to apply to an unfamiliar word. • I spell some identified commonly misspelt words from the Year 3 and 4-word list.
Composition	• I write a non-narrative using simple organisational devices such as headings and sub-headings. • In narrative writing, I develop resolutions and endings.	• I make improvements by proposing changes to grammar and vocabulary to improve consistency. *(The accurate use of pronouns in sentences/ tenses)* • I look at and discuss different models of writing, taking account of purpose and audience. • I plan my writing by discussing and recording ideas. *(timeline, flowchart, spider diagram, jottings)* • I write a narrative with a clear structure, setting, characters and plot. • I suggest improvement to my writing through assessing the writing with peers and through self-assessment.	• I identify structure, grammatical features and use of vocabulary for effect in texts. • I compose sentences using a wider range of structures linked to the grammar objectives. *(e.g. tenses – including present perfect/subordinate clauses/ co-ordinating conjunctions.* • I begin to organise paragraphs around a theme. *(Supported by planning then moving to independence)*

Year 3 (continued)

Aspect	Autumn	Spring	Summer
Grammar	▪ I use a range of sentences with more than one clause by using a wider range of conjunctions in my writing. *(when, if, because, although)* ▪ I recognise and use determiners 'a', 'an' and 'the' appropriately. *(an apple; a house; the yellow car /the an a)*	▪ I use the perfect form of verbs instead of the simple past. *(I have written it down so we can check what he said) (he has worked hard)* ▪ I understand the purpose of adverbs. ▪ I use adverbs effectively in my writing. ▪ I use conjunctions, adverbs and prepositions to express time and cause. *(the next thing, next, soon, so, before, after, during, in, because of)*	▪ Word choices are adventurous and carefully selected to add detail and to engage the reader. ▪ Detail is added by the expansion of noun phrases before and after the noun and with the use of adverbials.
Punctuation	▪ I begin to use inverted commas for some direct speech punctuation.	▪ I use apostrophes for possession with increasing accuracy including plural possession.	▪ Commas are sometimes used to mark clauses and phrases.

Year 4

Aspect	Autumn	Spring	Summer
Handwriting	▪ I use the diagonal and horizontal strokes that are needed to join letters. ▪ I understand which letters, when adjacent to one another, are best left un-joined. b/p/s/x	▪ I increase the legibility, consistency and quality of my handwriting: down strokes of letters are parallel and equidistant; lines of writing are spaced sufficiently so that the ascenders and descenders of letters do not touch.	
Spelling	▪ I use the first two or three letters of a word to check its spelling in a dictionary.	▪ I spell words with additional prefixes and suffixes and understand how to add them to root words. (– ation, ous, ion, ian) ▪ I use plural 's' and possessive 's' correctly. (The girls were playing football. The girls' football boots. The girl's football boots.)	▪ I recognise and spell additional homophones. (accept/except; whose/who's; whether/weather; peace/piece; medal/meddle) ▪ I spell identified commonly misspelt words from the Year 3 and 4 word list.
Composition	▪ I write from memory simple dictated sentences that include words and punctuation taught. ▪ My narrative writing is organised into clear sequences with more than a basic beginning, middle and end.	▪ I write a narrative with a clear structure, setting, characters and plot. ▪ I include key vocabulary and grammar choices that link to the style of writing. (e.g.: Scientific words/ historical words/ words that fit with the context, e.g. science fiction)	▪ I begin to open paragraphs with topic sentences and organise them around a theme. (Boxing up method independently; five-part story volcano; chunking their writing into paragraphs- they then use this to ensure they have accurate paragraphs and how to demarcate them). ▪ My endings are developed and close the narrative appropriately relating to the beginning or a change in a character.

Year 4 (continued)

Aspect	Autumn	Spring	Summer
Grammar	• I use a range of sentences with more than one clause- through use of conjunctions. • *'We put our umbrellas up when it rained' becomes 'When it rained, we put up our umbrellas.'*) • I use of a wider range of conjunctions, such as, although, however, despite, as well as: • I use the correct article 'a' or 'an'. • My sentences are often opened in different ways to create effects.	• I use appropriate nouns or pronouns within and across sentences to support cohesion and avoid repetition. (When I was writing about bees, the hive and the queen. I remembered to write 'they', 'it', and 'she' every other time, so that my writing was less repetitive). • I make improvements to my writing by proposing changes to grammar and vocabulary to improve consistency. (e.g. accurate use of pronouns in sentences; 'I forgot to put the comma after a fronted adverbial'; realise the spelling of proberbly is wrong). • I use fronted adverbials of place, time and manner, including the use of a comma. ('Later that day, I went shopping',	• I use expanded noun phrases with modifying adjectives. ('The strict teacher with curly hair.') • I use adverbs and prepositions to express time, place and cause. • I build cohesion within paragraphs through controlled use of tenses; subordinating and co-ordinating conjunctions. • I use standard English for verb inflections- instead of spoken forms. (We were- instead of we was, or I did instead of I done. He is/his instead of he's)
Punctuation	• All my sentences are correctly demarcated.	• I use the apostrophe for omission and possession. – (women's rights, boys' cloakroom) • I secure the use of punctuation in direct speech-, including a comma after the reporting clause. (The conductor shouted, "Sit down!")	• I almost always use commas for fronted adverbials.

Year 5

Aspect	Autumn	Spring	Summer
Handwriting	• I choose which shape of a letter to use when given choices and deciding, as part of my personal style, whether, or not, to join specific letters. • I choose the writing implement that is best suited for a task. (e.g. quick notes, letters).		
Spelling	• I form verbs with prefixes, for example, dis, de, mis, over and re. • I use the first three or four letters of a word to check spelling, meaning or both in a dictionary. • I begin to proof read my work for spelling and punctuation errors.	• I spell some words with 'silent' letter. *(e.g. knight, psalm, solemn)* • I convert nouns and adjectives into verbs by adding a suffix, for example, ate, ise, ify. • I distinguish between homophones and other words which are often confused. (guessed/guest; serial/cereal; bridal/bridle; altar/alter; desert/dessert; draft/draught; stationary/staitionery; principal/principle)	• I can spell identified commonly misspelt words from Year 5 and 6-word list. *(Draw on knowledge of root words e.g.: ordinary to spell extra ordinary/ordinarily)*
Compositio n	• My writing shows that I aim for a range of audiences and the purpose of my writing is to inform, entertain or persuade. • I organise writing into paragraphs to show different information or events. (TIP TOP – Time, Place, Topic, Person Speaking) (paragraphs can be extended or developed- main point, topic, event, idea with an explanation or additional detail)	• I link ideas within paragraphs. (connecting adverbs and adverbials for time (when); place (where); how (as/with) • I develop characters through action, description and dialogue. (Correct and effective use of speech, "Well done, you can use speech marks correctly!" exclaimed the teacher proudly. Description of action through well-chosen adjectives, verbs and adverbs). • I add well-chosen detail to interest the reader. (Expanded noun phrases-'the small playground with the horizontal climbing wall…; the north coast beaches with the best surf…; a tiny kitten with its eyes barely open...').	• My settings are used to not only create atmosphere, but also to indicate a change. • Models from my reading are often used or integrated into my writing. I manage shifts in time and place effectively and guide the reader through my text.

Year 5 (continued)

Aspect	Autumn	Spring	Summer
Grammar	▪ I ensure the correct and consistent use of tense throughout a piece of writing. ▪ I start sentences in different ways. *(-ed/-ing/simile openers, adverbials, conjunctions, not with the pronouns I, He, She, They, It, Him, Her etc. or The). (adverbials of time- Later, When the, As the dawn broke,) (adverbials of place-nearby, Inside, On top of, Over the rainbow, In a nearby village,) (manner- as quick as a flash, with legs swinging in the air,)* ▪ I use a thesaurus for alternative word choices.	▪ I use stylistic devices to create effects in writing. *(simile, metaphor, personification)* ▪ I use modal verbs or adverbs to indicate degrees of possibility. (There might be…. It could be….we may be…sometimes….possibly…. occasionally…) ▪ I use relative clauses beginning with who, which, where, when, whose, that or with an implied. (i.e. omitted) relative pronoun (Drop-in Sentence) ▪ I suggest changes to vocabulary, grammar and punctuation to enhance effects and clarify meaning.	▪ I use the perfect form of verbs to mark relationships of time and cause. (e.g. She has gone on holiday, and is not back yet. The coach has left without you, because you have just arrived late.) ▪ I choose words for deliberate effect and I use them thoughtfully and with precision.
Punctuation	▪ I use commas to clarify meaning or avoid ambiguity in writing.	▪ I use colons to introduce a list. ▪ I use inverted commas and other punctuation to accurately indicate direct speech.	▪ I use brackets, dashes or commas to indicate parenthesis. Outside I was smiling (Inside I was angrier than a bull about the charge).

Year 6

Aspect	Autumn	Spring	Summer
Handwriting	• I produce legible joined handwriting and develop my own personal fluent joined handwriting style. *(join/not join specific letters- loops)*		
Spelling	• I use a range of spelling strategies not just phonics. • I use a dictionary to check spelling/meaning. • I proof read and edit my work to check for spelling and punctuation errors. (Year 3 and 4 and Year 5/6 word lists) • I ensure I use the correct homophone. *(see Year 5/6 homophone list)* • I spell most words with silent letters.	• I change verbs into nouns by adding suffixes. (tion/sion/ment – cancel- cancellation/ expand- expansion/ excite- excitement/ enjoy- enjoyment)	• I make sure that I can spell the vast majority of words that appear in the Year 5/6 list.
Composition	• I use a thesaurus to develop word understanding and build a bank of antonyms and synonyms.	• I use paragraphs correctly so that each one has a clear topic, and has a signal of change in time, place or event. *(TIP TOP)* • I adapt the grammar and vocabulary used in my writing to suit the audience and purpose. (choose the appropriate form and register/ structure/ layout) • I create atmosphere and describe settings- I use antonyms and synonyms to enhance the description. • I describe and integrate dialogue to convey character and advance the action. (use of inverted commas, mostly correct) • I add detail to my writing by using expanded noun phrases to add precision, detail and qualification.	• My second drafts show evaluative and reflective thinking which is evidenced by thoughtful and effective changes made to create effects and to impact on the reader. • My writing is evaluated as a matter of course and proof reading ensures a high level of accuracy.

Year 6 (continued)

Aspect	Autumn	Spring	Summer
Grammar	▪ I use the correct tense throughout a piece of writing. ▪ I use modal verbs mostly appropriately to suggest degrees of possibility. (could, would, might) ▪ I add precision, detail and qualification using prepositional phrases and adverbs. ▪ I effectively draft my work so that I enhance meaning and adapt my grammar choices for effect.	▪ I use a range of cohesive devices*, including adverbials, within and across sentences and paragraphs. (Pronouns/ adverbials, conjunctions, similes, -ing, -ed, adverb openers/ repetition of key words for effect/ prepositional phrases/ tenses are secure/ellipses in narratives) ▪ I ensure correct subject verb agreement in singular and plural. e.g. was – I (one person) were – we (more than one- the children were) ▪ I use a wide range of clause structures, sometimes varying their position within the sentence. (*Relative clauses/ embedded clauses/subordinate and coordinating clauses/ adverbials/ prepositional clauses*). ▪ I use structures typical of very formal speech. (Subjunctive forms- If I were/ Were they to come, or questions tags- he is your friend, isn't he?)	▪ I use modal verbs and adverbs to position an argument as well as indicate degrees of possibility, probability and certainty. ▪ I use a range of verb forms to create more subtle meanings. ▪ I use the passive voice to present information with a different emphasis. (I broke the window in the greenhouse- The window of the greenhouse was broken (by me). ▪ My vocabulary choices are imaginative and words are used precisely and appropriately to create impact and enhance meaning.
Punctuation	▪ I can mostly use commas correctly to mark phrases and clauses- clarity.	▪ I make some correct use of a further range of punctuation across a range of writing. (Colons to start lists; semi colons to separate items in lists and hyphens to emphasis ideas/ use of semi colon/ colon to mark clauses- It's raining; I'm fed up) ▪ I can use punctuation for parenthesis, mostly correctly. (*brackets/commas/hyphens*)	

Key Assessment Criteria
Mathematics

Year 1

Aspect	Autumn	Spring	Summer
Number and Place Value	▪ I count to and across 100, forward and backward, beginning with 0 or 1, or from any given number. ▪ I count in multiples of 2s, 5s and 10s. ▪ I read and write numbers to 100 in numerals	▪ Given a number, I can identify 1 more or 1 less.	▪ I read and write numbers from 1 to 20 in numerals and words
Addition and Subtraction	▪ I read, write and interpret mathematical statements involving + - = signs. ▪ I represent and use number bonds and related subtractions facts within 20.	▪ I add and subtract 1-digit and 2-digit numbers to 20, including zero. ▪ I solve one-step problems that involve addition and subtraction, using concrete objects and pictorial representations, and missing number problems.	▪ I add and subtract 1-digit and 2-digit numbers to 20, including zero.
Multiplication and Division		▪ I solve one-step problems involving multiplication and division, by calculating the answer using concrete objects, pictorial representations and arrays with the support of my teacher.	
Fractions	▪ I recognise, find and name a half as one of two equal parts of an object, shape or quantity.	▪ I recognise, find and name a quarter as one of four equal parts of an object, shape or quantity.	

Year 1 (continued)

Aspect	Autumn	Spring	Summer
Measures	• I compare, describe and solve practical problems for: lengths and heights and mass/weight • I compare, describe and solve practical problems for: capacity and volume • I recognise and know the value of different denominations of coins and notes. • I sequence events in chronological order using language (e.g. before, after, next, first, today, yesterday, tomorrow, morning, afternoon, evening). • I recognise and use language relating to dates, including days of the week, weeks, months, years.	• I measure and begin to record the following: mass/weight. • I measure and begin to record the following: length and heights. • I compare, describe and solve practical problems for: time.	• I can measure and begin to record the following: capacity and volume. • I can tell the time to the hour and half past the hour and draw the hands on a clock face to show these times.
Geometry	• I recognise and name common 2D shapes, including circles and triangles.	• I identify and describe common 2D shapes, including: rectangles (including squares) circles, triangles. • I describe position, direction and movement, including half, quarter and three-quarter turns.	• I describe position, direction and movement, including half, quarter and three-quarter turns . • I recognise and name common 3D shapes, including: cuboids (including cubes), pyramids, spheres.

Year 2

Aspect	Autumn	Spring	Summer
Number and Place Value	• I count in steps of 2 and 5 from 0, and in tens from any number, forward and backward. • I read and write numbers to at least 100 in numerals and in words.	• I compare and order numbers from 0 up to 100; use < > and = signs.	• I recognise the place value of each digit in a 2-digit number. • I count in steps of 3 from 0, and in tens from any number, forward and backward.
Addition and Subtraction	• I recall and use addition and subtraction facts to 20 fluently and derive and use related facts up to 100. • I add and subtract numbers mentally, including: 2-digit numbers and ones; 2-digit numbers and tens; two 2-digit numbers; adding three 1-digit numbers.	• I understand that addition of any two numbers can be done in any order (commutative) and subtraction of one number from another cannot.	• I recognise and use the inverse relationship between addition and subtraction and use this to check calculations and missing number problems.
Multiplication and Division	• I recall and use multiplication and division facts for the 2, 5 and 10 tables, including recognising odd and even numbers.	• I calculate the mathematical statements for multiplication and division within the multiplication tables and write them using the x ÷ and = signs. • I understand that multiplication of two numbers can be one in any order (commutative) and division of one number by another cannot.	• I recognise that division is the inverse of multiplication and use to check calculations.
Fractions	• I recognise, find, name and write factions 1/3, 1/4, 2/4, 1/2, 3/4 of a length, shape, set of objects, or quantity.	• I write simple fractions and recognise the equivalence.	

Year 2 (continued)

Aspect	Autumn	Spring	Summer
Measures	▪ I compare and order lengths and mass, and record the results using >, < and =. ▪ I recognise and use symbols for pounds (£) and pence (p); combine amounts to make particular values. ▪ I tell and write the time to quarter past/to the hour and draw the hands on a clock face to show these times.	▪ I compare and order volume/capacity and record the results using >, < and =. ▪ I solve simple problems in a practical context involving addition and subtraction of money of the same unit, including giving change. ▪ I choose and use appropriate standard units to estimate and measure: length/height in any direction (m/cm); mass (kg/g) to the nearest appropriate unit, using rulers and scales. ▪ I tell and write the time to five minutes, including quarter past/to the hour and draw the hands on a clock face to show these times.	▪ I choose and use appropriate standard units to estimate and measure: temperature (°C); capacity (l/ml) to the nearest appropriate unit, using thermometers and measuring vessels. ▪ I compare and sequence intervals of time. ▪ I find different combinations of coins that equal the same amounts of money. ▪ I solve simple problems in a practical context involving addition and subtraction of money of the same unit, including giving change.
Geometry	▪ I identify and describe the properties of 2D shapes, including the number of sides and line symmetry in a vertical line. ▪ I identify and describe the properties of 3D shapes, including the number of edges, vertices and faces.	▪ I identify 2D shapes on the surface of 3D shapes. ▪ I order and arrange combinations of mathematical objects in patterns and sequences.	▪ I use mathematical vocabulary to describe position, direction and movement, including movement in a straight line distinguishing between rotation as a turn and in terms of right angles for quarter, half and three-quarter turns (clockwise and anti-clockwise). ▪ I compare and sort common 2D and 3D shapes and everyday objects.
Statistics	▪ I interpret and construct: pictograms; tally charts; block diagrams and simple tables.	▪ I ask and answer simple questions by counting the number of objects in each category and sorting the categories by quantity. ▪ I ask and answer questions about totalling and compare categorical data.	

Year 3

Aspect	Autumn	Spring	Summer
Number and Place Value	<ul><li>I count from 0 in multiples of 4, 8, 50 and 100.</li><li>I can find 10 or 100 more, or less, than a given number.</li><li>I read and write numbers to 1,000 in numerals and words</li></ul>	<ul><li>I compare and order numbers up to 1000.</li><li>I recognise the place value of each digit in a 3-digit number.</li></ul>	
Addition and Subtraction		<ul><li>I add and subtract numbers mentally, including: 3-digit number and ones; 3-digit numbers and tens; 3-digit numbers and hundreds.</li><li>I add and subtract numbers with up to 3 digits, using formal written methods of columnar addition and subtraction.</li></ul>	<ul><li>I estimate the answer to a calculation and use the inverse operations to check my answers.</li><li>I count up and down in tenths; recognise that tenths arise from dividing an object into ten equal parts and in dividing numbers or quantities by 10.</li><li>I add and subtract measures (length, mass and volume) with up to 3 digits, using formal written methods of columnar addition and subtraction.</li><li>I solve word problems including missing number problems, number facts, place value and more complex addition and subtraction.</li></ul>
Multiplication and Division	<ul><li>I recall and use the multiplication and division facts for the 3, 4 and 8 tables.</li><li>I write and calculate mathematical statements for multiplication using known multiplication tables, including 2-digit x 1-digit, using mental and progressing to formal written methods.</li><li>I write and calculate mathematical statements for division using known multiplication tables, including 2-digit x 1-digit, using mental and progressing to formal written methods.</li></ul>	<ul><li>I write and calculate mathematical statements for multiplication and division using known multiplication tables, including use of money and length.</li></ul>	<ul><li>I practise formal methods of multiplication and division, including a high focus on reasoning.</li></ul>

Year 3 (continued)

Aspect	Autumn	Spring	Summer
Fractions		▪ I recognise and show, using diagrams, equivalent fractions with small denominators. ▪ I recognise, find and write fractions of a discrete set of objects: unit fractions and non-unit fractions with small denominators. ▪ I compare and order unit fractions, and fractions with the same denominators. ▪ I add and subtract fractions with the same denominator within one whole.	
Measures	▪ I measure the perimeter of simple 2D shapes. ▪ I estimate and read time with increasing accuracy to the nearest minute; Tell and write the time from an analogue clock, including using Roman numerals from I to XII.	▪ I measure, compare, add and subtract: lengths (m/cm/mm); mass (kg/g); volume/ capacity (l/ml). ▪ I read 12-hour and 24-hour clocks. ▪ I record and compare time in terms of seconds, minutes, hours. ▪ I use vocabulary such as o'clock, am/pm, morning, afternoon, noon and midnight.	▪ I know the numbers of seconds in a minute and the number of days in each month, year and leap year. ▪ I compare durations of events, for example to calculate time taken by particular events or tasks.
Geometry	▪ I make 3D shapes using modelling materials; recognise 3D shapes in different orientations; and describe them.	▪ I draw 2D shapes. ▪ I recognise angles are a property of shape or a description of a turn. ▪ I identify right angles, recognise that two right angles make a half-turn, three make three quarters and four a complete turn ▪ I identify whether angles are greater than or less than a right angle.	▪ I identify horizontal and vertical lines and pairs of perpendicular and parallel lines.
Statistics	▪ I interpret and present data using: bar charts; pictograms and tables.		▪ I solve 1-step and 2-step questions such as 'How many more?' and 'How many fewer?' using information presented in scaled bar charts, pictograms and other graphs.

Year 4

Aspect	Autumn	Spring	Summer
Number and Place Value	<ul><li>I count backwards through zero to include negative numbers</li><li>I count in multiples of 6, 7, 9, 25 and 1000.</li></ul>	<ul><li>I read Roman numerals to 100 and understand that over time, the numeral system changes to include the concept of zero and place value.</li><li>I find 1000 more or less than a given number.</li></ul>	<ul><li>I compare and order numbers beyond 1000.</li><li>I round any number to the nearest 10, 100 or 1000.</li></ul>
Addition and Subtraction	<ul><li>I add and subtract numbers with up to 4 digits using the formal written methods of columnar addition and subtraction, where appropriate.</li><li>I estimate and use inverse operations to check answers to a calculation.</li></ul>		<ul><li>I solve addition and subtraction two-step problems in contexts, deciding which operations and methods to use and why.</li></ul>
Multiplication and Division	<ul><li>I recall multiplication and division facts for tables up to 12x12.</li><li>I recognise and use factor pairs and commutativity in mental calculations.</li><li>I multiply 2-digit and 3-digit numbers by a 1-digit number using formal written layout.</li></ul>	<ul><li>I divide 2-digit and 3-digit numbers by a 1-digit number using formal written layout with no remainder.</li><li>I use place value, known and derived facts to multiply and divide mentally, including multiplying by 0 and 1; multiplying three numbers together.</li><li>I find the effect of multiplying a number with up to 2 decimal places by 10 and 100, identifying the value of the digits in the answer as ones, tenths and hundredths.</li></ul>	

Year 4 (continued)

Aspect	Autumn	Spring	Summer
Fractions		• I recognise and show, using diagrams, families of common equivalent fractions. • I add and subtract fractions with the same denominator.	• I find the effect of dividing a 1-digit or 2-digit number by 10 and 100, identifying the value of the digits in the answer as ones, tenths and hundredths. • I count up and down in hundredths; recognise that hundredths arise from dividing an object into one 100 equal parts and in dividing numbers or quantities by 100. • I recognise and write decimals equivalents of any number of tenths or hundredths. • I recognise and write decimal equivalents to ¼, ½ and ¾. • I round decimals with one decimal place to the nearest whole number. • I compare numbers with the same number of decimal places up to two decimal places.
Measures	• I read, write and convert time between analogue and digital 12- and 24-hour clocks. • I measure and calculate the perimeter of a rectilinear figure (including squares) in cm and m.	• I find the area of rectilinear shapes by counting squares.	• I convert between different units of measure (e.g. km to m; hr to min).

Year 4 (continued)

Aspect	Autumn	Spring	Summer
Geometry	• I compare and classify geometric shapes, including quadrilaterals and triangles, based on their properties and sizes.	• I describe positions on a 2D grid as coordinates in the first quadrant. • I identify lines of symmetry in 2D shapes presented in different orientations. • I complete a simple symmetric figure with respect to a specific line of symmetry.	• I describe positions on a 2D grid as coordinates in the first quadrant. • I describe movements between positions as translations of a given unit to the left/right and up/down. • I plot specified points and draw sides to complete a given polygon. • I identify acute and obtuse angles, and compare and order angles up to two right angles by size.
Statistics	• I interpret and present discrete and continuous data using appropriate graphical methods, including: bar charts and time graphs.		• I solve comparison, sum and difference problems using information presented in bar charts, pictograms, tables and other graphs.

Year 5

Aspect	Autumn	Spring	Summer
Number and Place Value	▪ I count forward or backwards in steps of powers of 10 for any given number up to 1,000,000. ▪ I count up and down in thousandths; recognise that thousandths arise from dividing an object into 1000 equal parts and in dividing numbers or quantities by 1000.	▪ I interpret negative numbers in context, count forwards and backwards with positive and negative numbers, including through zero. ▪ I read Roman numerals to 1000 and recognise years written in Roman numerals.	▪ I read, write, order and compare numbers to at least 1,000,000 and determine the value of each digit. ▪ I round any number up to 1,000,000 to the nearest 10, 100, 1000, 10000 or 100000.
Addition and Subtraction	▪ I add and subtract numbers mentally with increasingly large numbers. ▪ I add and subtract whole numbers with more than 4 digits, including using formal written methods (columnar addition and subtraction).	▪ I use rounding to check answers to calculations and determine, in the context of a problem, levels of accuracy.	▪ I solve addition and subtraction multi-step problems in contexts, deciding which operations and methods to use and why.
Multiplication and Division	▪ I identify multiples and factors, including finding all factor pairs of a number, and common factors of two numbers. ▪ I multiply and divide numbers mentally drawing upon known facts. ▪ I know and use the vocabulary of prime numbers, prime factors and composite (non-prime) numbers and establish whether a number up to 100 is prime and recall prime numbers up to 19. ▪ I multiply numbers up to 4-digits by a 1-digit or 2-digit number using a formal written method, including long multiplication for 2-digit numbers.	▪ I divide numbers up to 4-digits by a 1-digit number using the formal written method of short division and interpret remainders appropriately for the context. ▪ I multiply and divide whole numbers and those involving decimals by 10, 100 and 1000. ▪ I solve problems involving multiplication and division using knowledge of factors and multiples, squares and cubes. ▪ I solve problems involving addition, subtraction, multiplication and division and a combination of these, including understanding of the equals sign.	▪ I recognise and use square numbers and cube numbers, and the notation for squared^2 and cubed^3. ▪ I solve problems involving multiplication and division including scaling by simple fractions and problems involving simple rates.

Year 5 (continued)

Aspect	Autumn	Spring	Summer
Fractions	• I identify, name and write equivalent fractions of a given fraction, represented visually, including tenths and hundredths. • I read and write decimal numbers as fractions, e.g. 0.71 = 71/100.	• I recognise mixed numbers and improper fractions and convert from one form to the other and write mathematical statements.	• I compare and order fractions whose denominators are all multiples of the same number. • I round decimals with two decimal places to the nearest whole number and to one decimal place. • I read, write, order and compare numbers with up to three decimal places. • I recognise the percent symbol (%) and understand that per cent relates to 'number of parts per hundred', and write percentages as a fraction with denominator 100, and as a decimal.
Measures	• I measure and calculate the perimeter of composite rectilinear shapes in cm and m. • I calculate and compare the area of rectangles (including squares), and including using standard units, square centimetres (cm²) and square metres (m²) and estimate the area of irregular shapes.	• I estimate volume (e.g. using 1 cm³ blocks to build cuboids, including cubes) and capacity (e.g. using water). • I convert between different units of metric measure (e.g. km/m; cm/m; cm/mm; g/kg; l/ml).	• I solve problems involving converting between units of time. • I understand and use approximate equivalences between metric units and common imperial units such as inches, pounds and pints.

Year 5 (continued)

Aspect	Autumn	Spring	Summer
Geometry	<ul><li>I know angles are measured in degrees;</li><li>I estimate and compare acute, obtuse and reflex angles.</li><li>I identify angles at a point on a straight line and ½ a turn (total 180°); and I identify angles at a point and one whole turn (total 360°); I identify other multiples of 90°;</li><li>I draw given angles, and measure them in degrees.</li></ul>	<ul><li>I identify, describe and represent the position of a shape following a reflection or translation, using the appropriate language and know that the shape has not changed.</li><li>I distinguish between regular and irregular polygons based on reasoning about equal sides and angles.</li><li>I identify 3D shapes, including cubes and other cuboids, from 2D representations.</li><li>I use the properties of rectangles to deduce related facts and find missing lengths and angles.</li></ul>	
Statistics	<ul><li>I complete, read and interpret information in: tables, including timetables</li></ul>	<ul><li>I solve comparison, addition and difference problems using information presented in a line graph.</li></ul>	

Year 6

Aspect	Autumn	Spring	Summer
Number and Place Value	▪ I read, write, order and compare numbers up to 10,000,000 and determine the value of each digit.	▪ I use negative numbers in context and calculate intervals across zero.	▪ I round any whole number to the required degree of accuracy. ▪ I solve number and practical problems that involve all other number and place value objectives.
Addition and Subtraction	▪ I perform mental calculations, including with mixed operations and large numbers. ▪ I use knowledge of the order of operations to carry our calculations involving the four operations. ▪ I use estimation to check answers to calculations and determine, in the context of a problem, levels of accuracy.	▪ I use knowledge of the order of operations to carry our calculations involving the four operations.	▪ I solve addition and subtraction multi-step problems in contexts, deciding which operations and methods to use and why. ▪ I solve problems involving addition, subtraction, multiplication and division.
Multiplication and Division	▪ I identify common factors, common multiples and prime numbers. ▪ I perform mental calculations, including with mixed numbers and large numbers.	▪ I multiply multi-digit numbers up to 4-digits by a 2-digit whole number using the formal written method of long multiplication. ▪ I divide numbers up to 4-digits by a 2-digit whole number using the formal written method of long division, and interpret remainders as whole number remainders, fractions, or by rounding, as appropriate for the context. ▪ I divide numbers up to 4-digits by a 2-digit number using the formal written method of short division, where appropriate, interpreting remainders according to the context.	• I solve multiplication and division multi-step problems in contexts, deciding which operations and methods to use and why.

Year 6 (continued)

Aspect	Autumn	Spring	Summer
Fraction	• I compare and order fractions, including fractions. • I use common factors to simplify fractions; use common multiples to express fractions in the same denomination. • I recall and use equivalences between simple fractions, decimals and percentages, including different contexts.	• I add and subtract fractions with different denominators and mixed numbers, using the concept of equivalent fractions.	• I multiply simple pairs of proper fractions, writing the answer in the simplest form. • I divide proper fractions by whole numbers. • I associate a fraction with division to calculate decimal fraction equivalents, for simple fractions.
Measures	• I calculate, estimate and compare volume of cubes and cuboids using standard units, including cm^3 and m^3, and extending to other units such as mm^3 and km^3. • I convert between miles and km. • I use, read, write and convert between standard units, converting measurements of length, mass, volume and time from a smaller unit of measure to a larger unit, and vice versa, using decimal notation to three decimal places.	• I solve problems involving the calculation and conversion of units of measure, using decimal notation to three decimal places where appropriate. • I recognise when it is possible to use formulae for area and volume of shapes.	• I recognise that shapes with the same areas can have different perimeters and vice versa. • I calculate the area of parallelograms and triangles.
Geometry	• I compare and classify geometric shapes based on their properties and sizes and find unknown angles in any triangles, quadrilaterals, and regular polygons. • I draw 2D shapes using given dimensions and angles.	• I describe positions on the full coordinate grid, (all four quadrants). • I draw and translate simple shapes on the coordinate plane, and reflect them in the axes. • I recognise, describe and build simple 3D shapes, including making nets.	• I recognise angles where they meet at a point, are on a straight line, or are vertically opposite, and find missing angles. • I illustrate and name parts of circles, including radius, diameter and circumference and know that the diameter is twice the radius.

Year 6 (continued)

Aspect	Autumn	Spring	Summer
Statistics		▪ I interpret and construct: pie charts and line graphs and use these to solve problems.	▪ I calculate and interpret the mean as an average
Ratio and Proportion		▪ I solve problems involving the relative sizes of two quantities where missing values can be found by using integer multiplication and division facts. ▪ I solve problems involving the calculation of percentages of whole numbers or measures such as 15% of 360 and the use of percentages for comparison.	
Algebra			▪ I express missing number problems algebraically and use simple formulae. ▪ I find pairs of numbers that satisfy number sentences with two unknowns.

Key Assessment Criteria
Speaking

A Year 1 speaker	A Year 2 speaker	A Year 3 speaker
• I speak clearly and confidently in front of people in my class. • I re-tell a well known story and remember the main characters. • I hold attention when playing and learning with others. • I keep to the main topic when we are talking in a group. • I ask questions in order to get more information. • I start a conversation with an adult I know well or with my friends. • I listen carefully to the things other people have to say in a group. • I join in with conversations in a group. • I join in with role play.	• I ask question to get more information and clarify meaning. • I talk in complete sentences. • I decide when I need to use specific vocabulary. • I take turns when talking in pairs or a small group. • I am aware that formal and informal situations require different language (beginning). • I retell a story using narrative language and linking words and phrases. • I hold the attention of people I am speaking to by adapting the way I talk. • I understand how to speak for different purposes and audiences (beginning). • I perform a simple poem from memory.	• I sequence and communicate ideas in an organised and logical way, always using complete sentences. • I vary the amount of detail and choice of vocabulary, depending on the purpose and the audience. • I take a full part in paired and group discussions. • I show that I know when Standard English is required and use it (beginning). • I retell a story using narrative language and add relevant detail. • I show that I have listened carefully because I make relevant comments. • I present ideas or information to an audience. • I recognise that meaning can be expressed in different ways, depending on the context. • I perform poems from memory adapting expression and tone as appropriate.

A Year 4 speaker	A Year 5 speaker	A Year 6 speaker
• I ask questions to clarify or develop my understanding. • I sequence, develop and communicate ideas in an organised and logical way, always using complete sentences. • I show that I understand the main point and the details in a discussion. • I adapt what I am saying to the needs of the listener or audience (increasingly). • I show that I know that language choices vary in different contexts. • I present to an audience using appropriate intonation; controlling the tone and volume so that the meaning is clear. • I justify an answer by giving evidence. • I use Standard English when it is required. • I perform poems or plays from memory, conveying ideas about characters and situations by adapting expression and tone.	• I engage the listener by varying my expression and vocabulary. • I adapt my spoken language depending on the audience, the purpose or the context. • I develop my ideas and opinions, providing relevant detail. • I express my point of view. • I show that I understand the main points, including implied meanings in a discussion. • I listen carefully in discussions. I make contributions and ask questions that are responsive to others' ideas and views. • I use Standard English in formal situations. • I am beginning to use hypothetical language to consider more than one possible outcome or solution. • I perform my own compositions, using appropriate intonation and volume so that meaning is clear. • I perform poems and plays from memory, making careful choices about how I convey ideas. I adapt my expression and tone. • I begin to select the appropriate register according to the context.	• I talk confidently and fluently in a range of situations, using formal and Standard English, if necessary. • I ask questions to develop ideas and take account of others' views. • I explain ideas and opinions giving reasons and evidence. • I take an active part in discussions and can take on different roles. • I listen to, and consider the opinions of, others in discussions. • I make contributions to discussions, evaluating others' ideas and respond to them. • I sustain and argue a point of view in a debate, using the formal language of persuasion. • I express possibilities using hypothetical and speculative language. • I engage listeners through choosing appropriate vocabulary and register that it is matched to the context. • I perform my own compositions, using appropriate intonation, volume and expression so that literal and implied meaning is clear. • I perform poems and plays from memory, making deliberate choices about how to convey ideas about characters, contexts and atmosphere.

Key Assessment Criteria
Science

A Year 1 scientist

Working scientifically (Y1 and Y2)

- I know how to ask simple scientific questions.
- I know how to use simple equipment to make observations.
- I know how to carry out simple tests.
- I know how to identify and classify things.
- I know how to explain to others what I have found out.
- I know how to use simple data to answer questions

Biology

Plants
- I know and name a variety of common wild and garden plants.
- I know and name the petals, stem, leaves and root of a plant.
- I know and name the roots, trunk, branches and leaves of a tree.

Animals, including humans
- I know and name a variety of animals including fish, amphibians, reptiles, birds and mammals.
- I classify and know animals by what they eat (carnivore, herbivore and omnivore).
- I know how to sort animals into categories (including fish, amphibians, reptiles, birds and mammals).
- I know how to sort living and non-living things.
- I know how to name the parts of the human body that I can see.
- I know how to link the correct part of the human body to each sense.

Chemistry

Everyday materials
- I distinguish between an object and the material it is made from.
- I know the materials that an object is made from.
- I know the difference between wood, plastic, glass, metal, water and rock.
- I know about the properties of everyday materials.
- I group objects based on the materials they are made from.

Physics

Seasonal changes
- I observe and know about the changes in the seasons.
- I name the seasons and know about the type of weather in each season.

A Year 2 scientist

Working scientifically (Y1 and Y2)	Biology	Chemistry	Physics
• I know how to ask simple scientific questions. • I know how to use simple equipment to make observations. • I know how to carry out simple tests. • I know how to identify and classify things. • I know how to explain to others what I have found out. • I know how to use simple data to answer questions	Living things and their habitats • I identify things that are living, dead and never lived. • I know how a specific habitat provides for the basic needs of things living there (plants and animals). • I identify and name plants and animals in a range of habitats. • I match living things to their habitat. • I know how animals find their food. • I name some different sources of food for animals. • I know and can explain a simple food chain. Plants • I know how seeds and bulbs grow into plants. • I know what plants need in order to grow and stay healthy (water, light & suitable temperature). Animals, including humans • I know the basic stages in a life cycle for animals, including humans. • I know what animals and humans need to survive. • I know why exercise, a balanced diet and good hygiene are important for humans.	Uses of everyday materials • I identify and name a range of materials, including wood, metal, plastic, glass, brick, rock, paper and cardboard. • I know why a material might or might not be used for a specific job. • I know how materials can be changed by squashing, bending, twisting and stretching.	No content

A Year 3 scientist

Working scientifically (Y3 and Y4)

- I know how to ask relevant scientific questions.
- I know how to use observations and knowledge to answer scientific questions.
- I know how to set up a simple enquiry to explore a scientific question.
- I know how to set up a test to compare two things.
- I know how to set up a fair test and explain why it is fair.
- I make careful and accurate observations, including the use of standard units.
- I know how to use equipment, including thermometers and data loggers to make measurements.
- I gather, record, classify and present data in different ways to answer scientific questions.
- I know how to use diagrams, keys, bar charts and tables; using scientific language.
- I know how to use findings to report in different ways, including oral and written explanations, presentation.
- I know how to draw conclusions and suggest improvements.
- I know how to make a prediction with a reason.
- I know how to identify differences, similarities and changes related to an enquiry.

Biology

Plants
- I know the function of different parts of flowing plants and trees.
- I know what different plants need to help them survive.
- I know how water is transported within plants.
- I know the plant life cycle, especially the importance of flowers.

Animals, including humans
- I know about the importance of a nutritious, balanced diet.
- I know how nutrients, water and oxygen are transported within animals and humans.
- I know about the skeletal system of a human.
- I know about the muscular system of a human.
- I know about the purpose of the skeleton in humans and animals.

Chemistry

Rocks
- I compare and group rocks based on their appearance and physical properties, giving a reason.
- I know how fossils are formed.
- I know how soil is made.
- I know about and explain the difference between sedimentary, metamorphic and igneous rock.

Physics

Light
- I know what dark is (the absence of light).
- I know that light is needed in order to see.
- I know that light is reflected from a surface.
- I know and demonstrate how a shadow is formed.
- I explore shadow size and explain the changes.
- I know the danger of direct sunlight and describe how to keep protected.

Forces and magnets
- I know about and describe how objects move on different surfaces.
- I know how some forces require contact and some do not, giving examples.
- I know about and explain how objects attract and repel in relation to objects and other magnets.
- I predict whether objects will be magnetic and carry out an enquiry to test this out.
- I know how magnets work.
- I predict whether magnets will attract or repel and give a reason.

A Year 4 scientist

Working scientifically (Y3 and Y4)	Biology	Chemistry	Physics
• I know how to ask relevant scientific questions. • I know how to use observations and knowledge to answer scientific questions. • I know how to set up a simple enquiry to explore a scientific question. • I know how to set up a test to compare two things. • I know how to set up a fair test and explain why it is fair. • I make careful and accurate observations, including the use of standard units. • I know how to use equipment, including thermometers and data loggers to make measurements. • I gather, record, classify and present data in different ways to answer scientific questions. • I know how to use diagrams, keys, bar charts and tables; using scientific language. • I know how to use findings to report in different ways, including oral and written explanations, presentation. • I know how to draw conclusions and suggest improvements. • I know how to make a prediction with a reason. • I know how to identify differences, similarities and changes related to an enquiry.	**Living things and their habitats** • I group living things in different ways. • I use classification keys to group, identify and name living things. • I create classification keys to group, identify and name living things (for others to use). • I know how changes to an environment could endanger living things. **Animals, including humans** • I identify and name the parts of the human digestive system. • I know the functions of the organs in the human digestive system. • I identify and know the different types of teeth in humans. • I know the functions of different human teeth. • I use food chains to identify producers, predators and prey. • I construct food chains to identify producers, predators and prey.	**States of matter** • I group materials based on their state of matter (solid, liquid, gas). • I know how some materials can change state. • I explore how materials change state. • I measure the temperature at which materials change state. • I know about the water cycle. • I know the part played by evaporation and condensation in the water cycle.	**Sound** • I know how sound is made. • I know how sound travels from a source to our ears. • I know how sounds are made, associating some of them with vibrating. • I know the correlation between pitch and the object producing a sound. • I know the correlation between the volume of a sound and the strength of the vibrations that produced it. • I know what happens to a sound as it travels away from its source. **Electricity** • I identify and name appliances that require electricity to function. • I construct a series circuit. • I identify and name the components in a series circuit (including cells, wires, bulbs, switches and buzzers). • I know how to draw a circuit diagram. • I predict and test whether a lamp will light within a circuit. • I know the function of a switch in a circuit. • I know the difference between a conductor and an insulator; giving examples of each.

A Year 5 scientist

Working scientifically (Y5 and Y6)

- I know how to plan different types of scientific enquiry.
- I know how to control variables in an enquiry.
- I measure accurately and precisely using a range of equipment.
- I know how to record data and results using scientific diagrams and labels, classification keys, tables, scatter graphs, bar and line graphs.
- I use the outcome of test results to make predictions and set up a further comparative and fair tests.
- I report findings from enquiries in a range of ways.
- I know how to explain a conclusion from an enquiry.
- I explain causal relationships in an enquiry.
- I know how to relate the outcome from an enquiry to scientific knowledge in order to state whether evidence supports or refutes an argument or theory.
- I read, spell and pronounce scientific vocabulary accurately.

Biology

Living things and their habitats

- I know the life cycle of different living things, e.g. mammal, amphibian, insect bird.
- I know the differences between different life cycles.
- I know the process of reproduction in plants.
- I know the process of reproduction in animals.

Animals, including humans

- I create a timeline to indicate stages of growth in humans.

Chemistry

Properties and changes of materials

- I compare and group materials based on their properties (e.g. hardness, solubility, transparency, conductivity, [electrical & thermal], and response to magnets).
- I know how a material dissolves to form a solution; explaining the process of dissolving.
- I know and show how to recover a substance from a solution.
- I know how some materials can be separated.
- I demonstrate how materials can be separated (e.g. through filtering, sieving and evaporating).
- I know and can demonstrate that some changes are reversible and some are not.
- I know how some changes result in the formation of a new material and that this is usually irreversible.
- I know about reversible and irreversible changes.
- I give evidenced reasons why materials should be used for specific purposes.

Physics

Earth and space

- I know about and explain the movement of the Earth and other planets relative to the Sun.
- I know about and explain the movement of the Moon relative to the Earth.
- I know and demonstrate how night and day are created.
- I describe the Sun, Earth and Moon (using the term spherical).

Forces

- I know what gravity is and its impact on our lives.
- I identify and know the effect of air resistance.
- I identify and know the effect of water resistance.
- I identify and know the effect of friction.
- I explain how levers, pulleys and gears allow a smaller force to have a greater effect.

A Year 6 scientist

Working scientifically (Y5 and Y6)	Biology	Chemistry	Physics
• I know how to plan different types of scientific enquiry. • I know how to control variables in an enquiry. • I measure accurately and precisely using a range of equipment. • I know how to record data and results using scientific diagrams and labels, classification keys, tables, scatter graphs, bar and line graphs. • I use the outcome of test results to make predictions and set up a further comparative and fair tests. • I report findings from enquiries in a range of ways. • I know how to explain a conclusion from an enquiry. • I explain causal relationships in an enquiry. • I know how to relate the outcome from an enquiry to scientific knowledge in order to state whether evidence supports or refutes an argument or theory. • I read, spell and pronounce scientific vocabulary accurately.	<u>Living things and their habitats</u> • I classify living things into broad groups according to observable characteristics and based on similarities & differences. • I know how living things have been classified. • I give reasons for classifying plants and animals in a specific way. <u>Animals, including humans</u> • I identify and name the main parts of the human circulatory system. • I know the function of the heart, blood vessels and blood. • I know the impact of diet, exercise, drugs and life style on health. • I know the ways in which nutrients and water are transported in animals, including humans. <u>Evolution and inheritance</u> • I know how the Earth and living things have changed over time. • I know how fossils can be used to find out about the past. • I know about reproduction and offspring (recognising that offspring normally vary and are not identical to their parents). • I know how animals and plants are adapted to suit their environment. • I link adaptation over time to evolution. • I know about evolution and can explain what it is.	No content	<u>Light</u> • I know how light travels. • I know and demonstrate how we see objects. • I know why shadows have the same shape as the object that casts them. • I know how simple optical instruments work, e.g. periscope, telescope, binoculars, mirror, magnifying glass etc. <u>Electricity</u> • I know how the number & voltage of cells in a circuit links to the brightness of a lamp or the volume of a buzzer. • I compare and give reasons for why components work and do not work in a circuit. • I draw circuit diagrams using correct symbols.

Explaining Working Scientifically – Year 1

	Examples (Typically Year 1)

I know how to ask simple scientific questions.	• I ask questions such as:
	  • Why are flowers different colours?
	  • Why do some animals eat meat and others not?

I know how to use simple equipment to make observations.	• I use a hand lens to see things more clearly. • I use binoculars to help me see animals that are in the distance.
I know how to carry out simple tests.	• I set up a test to see which materials keeps things warmest. • I know if my test has been successful and can say what I have learned.
I know how to identify and classify things.	• I group things according to a criteria I have been asked to consider, e.g., animals and plants.
I know how to explain to others what I have found out.	• I explain to someone what I have learnt from an investigation I have been involved with. • I draw conclusions from the answers to the questions I have asked.
I know how to use simple data to answer questions.	• I use measures (within Year 1 mathematical limits) to help me find out more about the investigations I am considering.

Explaining Working Scientifically – Year 2

	Examples (Typically Year 2)

I know how to ask simple scientific questions.	• I ask questions such as:
	  • Why do some trees lose their leaves in Autumn and others do not?
	  • How long are roots of tall trees?
	  • Why do some animals have underground habitats?

I know how to use simple equipment to make observations.	• I use equipment such as thermometers and rain gauges to help observe changes to my local environment as the year progresses. • I use microscopes that have been created for my age group to find out more about small creatures and plants.
I know how to carry out simple tests.	• With help, I find out how old a tree is. • I know how to set up a fair test and do so when finding out about how seeds grow best.
I know how to identify and classify things.	• I group things according to a given criteria, e.g., deciduous and coniferous trees. • I classify items such as toys according to the materials used to make them.
I know how to explain to others what I have found out.	• I explain to someone why my investigation is fair. • I draw conclusions from my fair tests and can explain what I have found out.
I know how to use simple data to answer questions.	• I use measures (within Year 2 mathematical limits) to help me find out more about the investigations I am engaged with.

Explaining Working Scientifically – Year 3 (Part 1)

I know how to ask relevant scientific questions.	• I ask questions such as: • Why does the moon appear in different shapes in the night sky? • Why does my shadow change during the day? • Where does a fossil come from?
I Know how to use observations and knowledge to answer scientific questions.	• I observe at what time of day my shadow is likely to be at its longest and shortest. • I observe which type of plants grow in different places, e.g., bluebells in woodland, roses in domestic gardens, etc.
I know how to set up a simple enquiry to explore a scientific question.	• I use research to find out how reflection can help me see things that are around the corner. • I use research to find out what the main differences are between sedimentary and igneous rocks
I know how to set up a test to compare two things.	• I test to see which type of soil is most suitable when growing two similar plants. • I test to see if my right hand is as efficient as my left hand.
I know how to set up a fair test and explain why it is fair.	• I set up a fair test with different variables, e.g., the best conditions for a plant to grow. • I explain to my partner why a test I have set up is a fair one, e.g., lifting weights with my right and left hand.
I know how to make careful and accurate observations, including the use of standard units.	• I measure carefully (taking account of mathematical knowledge up to Year 3) and add to my scientific learning.
I know how to use equipment, including thermometers and data loggers to make measurements.	• I use a data logger to check on the lightness and darkness of a room. • I use a thermometer to measure temperature and know there are two main scales used to measure temperature.

Working Scientifically – Year 3 (Part 2)

I know how to gather, record, classify and present data in different ways to answer scientific questions.	• I gather and record information using a chart, matrix or tally chart, depending on what is most sensible. • I group information according to common factors, e.g., plants that grow in woodlands or plants that grow in our gardens.
I know how to use diagrams, keys, bar charts and tables; using scientific language.	• I use bar charts and other statistical tables (in line with Year 3 mathematics statistics) to record my findings. • I know how to use a key to help me understand information presented on a chart. • I use correct scientific language when presenting information.
I know how to use findings to report in different ways, including oral and written explanations, presentation.	• I am confident enough to stand in front of others and explain what I have found out, for example about how the moon changes shape or how fossils help us to understand more about our planet. • I present my findings using written explanations and include diagrams when needed. • I work with a small group to present findings to others in the class.
I know how to draw conclusions and suggest improvements.	• I make sense of my findings and draw conclusions which helps me understand more about scientific information. • I make suggestions about how things could be improved.
I know how to make a prediction with a reason.	• When I make a prediction there is a plausible reason as to why I have done so. • I am able to amend my prediction according to my findings.
I know how to identify differences, similarities and changes related to an enquiry.	• I understand why the joints in my body need to be different even though they do a similar job. • I understand why the day and night are different lengths at different times of the year. • I am prepared to change my ideas as a result of what I have found out during a scientific enquiry.

Explaining Working Scientifically – Year 4 (Part 1)

I know how to ask relevant scientific questions.	• I ask questions such as:
	    • Why are steam and ice the same thing?
	    • Why is liver important in our digestive systems?
	    • What do we mean by 'pitch' when it comes to sound?

I Know how to use observations and knowledge to answer scientific questions.	• I notice that the further away you are from the source of sound the quieter the sound becomes. • I notice that on sunny days puddles on the playground disappear much quicker than they do on dull days.
I know how to set up a simple enquiry to explore a scientific question.	• I use research to find out how much time it takes to digest most of our food. • I use research to find out which materials make effective conductors and insulators of electricity.
I know how to set up a test to compare two things.	• I test to see which of two instruments make the highest or lowest sounds. • I test to see if a glass of ice weighs the same as a glass of water.
I know how to set up a fair test and explain why it is fair.	• I set up a fair test with more than one variable, e.g., using different materials to cut out sound. • I explain to other in my class why a test I have set up is a fair one, e.g., discover how fast ice melts in different temperatures.
I know how to make careful and accurate observations, including the use of standard units.	• I measure carefully (taking account of mathematical knowledge up to Year 4) and add to my scientific learning.
I know how to use equipment, including thermometers and data loggers to make measurements.	• I use a data logger to check on the time it takes ice to melt to water in different temperatures. • I use a thermometer to measure temperature and know there are two main scales used to measure temperature.

Explaining Working Scientifically – Year 4 (Part 2)

I know how to gather, record, classify and present data in different ways to answer scientific questions.	• I gather and record information using a chart, matrix or tally chart, depending on what is most sensible. • I group information according to common factors, e.g., materials that make goof conductors or insulators.
I know how to use diagrams, keys, bar charts and tables; using scientific language.	• I use bar charts and other statistical tables (in line with Year 4 mathematics statistics) to record my findings. • I know how to use a key to help me understand information presented on a chart. • I use correct scientific language when presenting information.
I know how to use findings to report in different ways, including oral and written explanations, presentation.	• I am confident enough to stand in front of others and explain what I have found out, for example about we digest our food. • I present my findings using written explanations and include diagrams when needed. • I write up my findings using a planning, doing and evaluating process.
I know how to draw conclusions and suggest improvements.	• I make sense of my findings and draw conclusions which helps me understand more about the scientific information I have learned. • I am confident enough to make suggestions about how things could be improved.
I know how to make a prediction with a reason.	• When I make a prediction there is a plausible reason as to why I have done so. • I am able to amend my prediction according to my findings.
I know how to identify differences, similarities and changes related to an enquiry.	• I understand why the digestive systems needs various organs. • I understand why the sound we hear travels on vibrations. • I am prepared to change my ideas as a result of what I have found out during a scientific enquiry.

Explaining Working Scientifically – Year 5 (Part 1)

I know how to plan different types of scientific enquiry.	• I set up an investigation when it is appropriate, e.g., finding out which materials dissolve or not. • I set up a fair test when needed, e.g., which surfaces create most friction? • I set up an enquiry based investigation, e.g., find out what we can do now that we couldn't do as a baby.
I know how to control variables in an enquiry.	• I know what the variables are in a given enquiry and can isolate each one when investigating, e.g., finding out how effective parachutes with different materials are.
I know how to measure accurately and precisely using a range of equipment.	• I use all measurements as set out in Year 5 mathematics (measurement), this includes capacity and mass. • I use other scientific instruments as needed, e.g., thermometer, rain gauge, spring scales (for measuring newtons)
I know how to record data and results using scientific diagrams and labels, classification keys, tables, scatter graphs, bar and line graphs.	• During my investigations, I am able to record data and present them in a range of ways including, diagrams, labels, classification keys, tables, scatter graphs and bar and line graphs. • I appreciate which format to use for different systems.
I know how to use the outcome of test results to make predictions and set up a further comparative and fair tests.	• I am confident using data which I have generated to help make sense of my investigations. • I make predictions based on information gleaned from my investigations. • I create new investigations which take account of what I have learned previously.

Explaining Working Scientifically – Year 5 (Part 2)

I know how to report findings from enquiries in a range of ways.	• I am able to present information related to my scientific enquiries in a range of ways including using IT such as power-point and iMovie. • I use a range of written methods to report my findings. • I use diagrams, as and when necessary, to support my writing. • I am confident enough to present my findings orally in front of the class.
I know how to explain a conclusion from an enquiry.	• I am evaluative when explaining my findings from my scientific enquiry. • I am clear about what I have found out from my enquiry and can relate this to others.
I know how to explain causal relationships in an enquiry.	• My explanations set out clearly why something has happened and its possible impact on other things. • I am able to relate causal relationships when studying life cycles.
I know how to relate the outcome from an enquiry to scientific knowledge in order to state whether evidence supports or refutes an argument or theory.	• I am aware of the need to support my conclusions with evidence. • I am able to give an example of something I have focused on when supporting a scientific theory, e.g., how much easier it is to lift a heavy object using pulleys.
I know how to read, spell and pronounce scientific vocabulary accurately.	• I keep an on-going record of new scientific words that I have come across for the first time. • I frequently carry out research when investigating a scientific principle or theory.

Explaining Working Scientifically – Year 6 (Part 1)

I know how to plan different types of scientific enquiry.	• I know which type of investigation is needed to suit my scientific enquiry, e.g., looking at the relationship between my pulse and exercise. • I set up a fair test when needed, e.g., does light travel in straight lines? • I know how to set up an enquiry based investigation, e.g., what is the relationship between oxygen and blood?.
I know how to control variables in an enquiry.	• I know what the variables are in a given enquiry and can isolate each one when investigating. • I justify which variable I have isolated in my scientific investigation.
I know how to measure accurately and precisely using a range of equipment.	• I use all measurements as set out in Year 6 mathematics (measurement), this includes capacity, mass, ratio and proportion. • I use other scientific instruments as needed, e.g., thermometer, rain gauge,
I know how to record data and results using scientific diagrams and labels, classification keys, tables, scatter graphs, bar and line graphs.	• During my investigations, I am able to record data and present them in a range of ways including, diagrams, labels, classification keys, tables, scatter graphs and bar and line graphs. • I appreciate which format to use for different systems.
I know how to use the outcome of test results to make predictions and set up a further comparative and fair tests.	• I am confident using data which I have generated to help make sense of my investigations. • I make accurate predictions based on information gleaned from my investigations. • I create new investigations which take account of what I have found out previously.

Explaining Working Scientifically – Year 6 (Part 2)

I know how to report findings from enquiries in a range of ways.	• I am able to present information related to my scientific enquiries in a range of ways including using IT such as power-point, animoto and iMovie. • I use a range of written methods to report my findings, including focusing on the planning, doing and evaluating phases. • I use diagrams, as and when necessary, to support my writing and I am confident enough to present my findings orally in front of the class.
I know how to explain a conclusion from an enquiry.	• I am evaluative when explaining my findings from my scientific enquiry. • I am clear about what I have found out from my enquiry and can relate this to others in my class.
I know how to explain causal relationships in an enquiry.	• My explanations set out clearly why something has happened and its possible impact on other things. • I am able to relate causal relationships when studying life cycles.
I know how to relate the outcome from an enquiry to scientific knowledge in order to state whether evidence supports or refutes an argument or theory.	• I am aware of the need to support my conclusions with evidence. • I am able to give an example of something I have focused on when supporting a scientific theory, e.g., classifying vertebrate and invertebrate creatures or why certain creatures choose their unique habitats.
I know how to read, spell and pronounce scientific vocabulary accurately.	• I keep an on-going record of new scientific words that I have come across for the first time and use these regularly in my scientific write ups. • I frequently carry out research when investigating a scientific principle or theory.

Key Assessment Criteria
Humanities

Assessing History at Key Stage 2

Please note:

- On the following two pages the **chronological** aspect of history has been set out assuming that:
  - Year 3 covers the Stone Age;
  - Year 4, the Romans;
  - Year 5, the Anglo-Saxons, and
  - Year 6, the Vikings.

- These elements have been highlighted. If you cover these periods of history in a different year group then you can inter-change the highlighted objectives to fit in with the chosen year group.

- In addition the assumption has been made that the Ancient Greeks are covered in Year 3. The key assessment criteria for this period could be moved to another age group if it was covered there instead.

A Year 1 historian	A Year 2 historian	A Year 3 historian
• I know about and can name many of the changed that have happened since I was born. • I know how to ask and answer questions about old and new objects, • I use words and phrases like: old, new and a long time ago. • I spot old and new things in a picture. • I use words and phrases like: before, after, past, present, then and now. • I give examples of things that were different when my grandparents were children. • I know about someone famous who was born or lived near our town. • I know why there is a monument to a famous person or event in the town centre.	• I know about an event that happened before my grandparents were born. • I recount the life of someone famous from Britain who lived in the past and I know about what they did to make the world a better place. • I recount the life of someone famous who lived outside Britain and explain why s/he was famous. • I know about the life of a famous person from the past because I know how to research. • I know how to use books and the internet to find out more information about the past. • I know how to find out things about the past by talking to an older person. • I know about how things were different when my grandparents were children. • I know what certain objects from the past might have been used for.	**• I know about how stone age people hunted for their food and what they ate.** **• I know about many of the differences between the stone, bronze and iron ages.** **• I know what people learnt from stone aged paintings.** **• I am able to describe what a typical day would have been like for a stone age man, woman or child.** ***The Greeks*** • I know about and can talk about the struggle between the Athenians and the Spartans. • I know about some of the things that the Greeks gave the world. • I know that the Greeks were responsible for the birth of the Olympics. • I know that the Greek Gods were an important part of Greek culture. • I know how to locate Greece on a map.

A Year 4 historian	A Year 5 historian	A Year 6 historian
• **I know about at least three things that the Romans did for our country.** • **I know why the Romans needed to build forts in this country.** • **I know that Rome was a very important place and many decisions were made there.** • **I know about the lives of at least two famous Romans.** • I know that there were many advanced civilizations on Earth 3000 years ago. • I summarise how Britain may have learnt from other countries and civilizations (historically and more recently). • I research to find answers to specific historical questions about our locality. • I research what it was like for children in a given period of history and present my findings to an audience. • I know how our locality today has been shaped by what happened in the past. • I know how historic items and artefacts have been used to help build up a picture of life in the past. • I know about the impact that one of these periods of history had on the world.	• **I know where the Anglo-Saxons came from.** • **I know at least two famous Anglo-Saxons** • **I use a time line to show when the Anglo-Saxons were in England** • **I know the link between Anglo-Saxons and Christianity.** • **I know that many Anglo-Saxons were farmers.** • **I know that the Anglo-Saxons gave us many of the words that we use today.** • I describe events from the past using dates when things happened. • I know how an event or events from the past has shaped our life today. • I draw a timeline with different historical periods showing key historical events or lives of significant people • I know how crime and punishment has changed over a period of time. • I know how Britain has had a major influence on the world. • I know how the lives of wealthy people were different from the lives of poorer people.	• **I know that Britain was invaded on more than one occasion.** • **I know that the Anglo-Saxons and Vikings were often in conflict.** • **I know how to use a timeline to show when the Vikings raids started.** • **I know why the Vikings often overpowered the Anglo-Saxons.** • **I show on a map where the Vikings came from and where they invaded our country.** • **I know that many Vikings came to our country as peaceful farmers.** • I research in order to find similarities and differences between two or more periods of history. • I know how to place features of historical events and people from the past societies and periods in a chronological framework. • I know about the main events from a period of history, explaining the order of events and what happened. • I know that many of the early civilizations gave much to the world.

A Year 1 geographer	A Year 2 geographer	A Year 3 geographer
• I know the names of the four countries in the United Kingdom and locate them on a map. • I know the names of the three main seas that surround the United Kingdom. • I keep a weather chart and answer questions about the weather. • I know about some of the main things that are in hot and cold places. • I know which clothes I would wear in hot and cold places. • I know how the weather changes throughout the year and name the seasons. • I point to the equator, North and South Pole on an atlas and globe. • I know about some of the features of an island. • I know where I live and tell someone my address. • I know the four main directions on a compass are North; East, South and West. • I know what I like and do not like about the place I live.	• I name the continents of the world and locate them on a map. • I name the world's oceans and locate them on a map. • I name the capital cities of England, Wales, Scotland and Northern Ireland. • I know what I like and do not like about a place that is different to the one I live in. • I describe a place outside Europe using geographical words. • I know how jobs may be different in other locations. • I know the key features of a place from a picture using words like beach, coast, forest, hill, mountain, ocean, valley. • I know about the facilities that a village, town and city may need and give reasons. • I use the directional vocabulary: near; far; left; right to explain where a location is.	• I know the name of a number of countries in the northern hemisphere. • I know the capital city of at least six European countries. • I locate the Tropic of Cancer, the Tropic of Capricorn and the Greenwich meridian on a map. • I know whether a country is located in the Southern or Northern hemisphere • I know why people may be attracted to live in cities. • I know why people may choose to live in one place rather than another. • I know about, locate and name some of the world's most famous volcanoes. • I know about and describe the key aspects of earthquakes. • I know about and describe the key aspects of volcanoes.

A Year 4 geographer	A Year 5 geographer	A Year 6 geographer
• I know how to plan a journey from my town/ city to another place in England.	• I know, name and locate the capital cities of neighbouring European countries.	• I know how to use an atlas by using the index to find places.
• I know how to find at least six cities in the UK on a map.	• I know the countries that make up the European Union.	• I know how to use some basic Ordnance Survey map symbols.
• I research to discover features of villages, towns and cities and appreciate the differences.	• I know about, name and locate many of the world's most famous mountainous regions.	• I know how to use Ordnance Survey symbols and six-figure grid references.
• I know about, name and locate some of the main islands that surround the United Kingdom.	• I know why most cities as situated by rivers.	• I collect and accurately measure information (e.g. rainfall, temperature, wind speed, noise levels etc).
• I know the areas of origin of the main ethnic groups in the United Kingdom and in our school.	• I know about the course of a river.	
	• I name and locate many of the world's most famous rivers.	• I know why some places are similar and dissimilar in relation to their human and physical features.
• I know the difference between the British Isles, Great Britain and the United Kingdom.	• I know why ports are important and the role they play in distributing goods around the world.	• I know how time zones work and calculate time differences around the world.
• I can use a road map to plan a journey from one city or town to another.	• I know what is meant by a biome.	• I name the largest deserts in the world and locate desert regions in an atlas.

Key Assessment Criteria
Creative Arts

A Year 1 artist	A Year 2 artist	A Year 3 artist
• I know how to show how people feel in paintings and drawings. • I know how to create moods in art work. • I know how to use pencils to create lines of different thickness in drawings. • I name the primary and secondary colours. • I know how to create a repeating pattern in print. • I know how to cut, roll and coil materials. • I know how to use IT to create a picture. • I describe what I can see and give an opinion about the work of an artist. • I ask questions about a piece of art.	• I choose and use three different grades of pencil when drawing. • I know how to use charcoal, pencil and pastel to create art. • I know how to use a viewfinder to focus on a specific part of an artefact before drawing it. • I know how to mix paint to create all the secondary colours. • I know how to create brown with paint. • I know how to create tints with paint by adding white. • I know how to create tones with paint by adding black. • I know how to create a printed piece of art by pressing, rolling, rubbing and stamping. • I know how to make a clay pot. • I know how to join two clay finger pots together. • I know how to use different effects within an IT paint package. • I suggest how artists have used colour, pattern and shape. • I know how to create a piece of art in response to the work of another artist.	• I know how to show facial expressions in my art. • I know how to use sketches to produce a final piece of art. • I know how to use different grades of pencil to shade and to show different tones and textures. • I know how to create a background using a wash. • I know how to use a range of brushes to create different effects in painting. • I know how to identify the techniques used by different artists. • I know how to use digital images and combine with other media in my art. • I know how to use IT to create art which includes my own work and that of others. • I know how to compare the work of different artists. • I recognise when art is from different cultures. • I recognise when art is from different historical periods.

A Year 4 artist	A Year 5 artist	A Year 6 artist
• I know how to show facial expressions and body language in sketches and paintings. • I know how to use marks and lines to show texture in my art. • I know how to use line, tone, shape and colour to represent figures and forms in movement. • I know how to show reflections in my art. • I know how to print onto different materials using at least four colours. • I know how to sculpt clay and other mouldable materials. • I know how to integrate my digital images into my art. • I experiment with the styles used by other artists. • I explain some of the features of art from historical periods.	• I identify and draw objects and use marks and lines, to produce texture. • I know how to successfully use shading to create mood and feeling. • I know how to organise line, tone, shape and colour to represent figures and forms in movement. • I know how to use shading to create mood and feeling. • I know how to express emotion in my art. • I know how to create an accurate print design following criteria. • I know how to use images which I have created, scanned and found; altering them where necessary to create art. • I research the work of an artist and use their work to replicate a style.	• I explain why I have used different tools to create art. • I explain why I have chosen specific techniques to create my art. • I explain the style of my work and how it has been influenced by a famous artist. • I know how to overprint to create different patterns. • I know how to use feedback to make amendments and improvement to my art. • I know how to use a range of e-resources to create art.

A Year 1 musician	A Year 2 musician	A Year 3 musician
• I know how to use my voice to speak, sing and chant. • I know how to use instruments to perform. • I know how to clap short rhythmic patterns. • I know how to make different sounds with my voice and with instruments. • I know how to repeat short rhythmic and melodic patterns. • I know how to make a sequence of sounds. • I know how to respond to different moods in music. • I know how to say whether I like or dislike a piece of music. • I know how to choose sounds to represent different things. • I know how to follow instructions about when to play and sing.	• I know how to sing and follow a melody. • I know how to perform simple patterns and accompaniments keeping a steady pulse. • I know how to play simple rhythmic patterns on an instrument. • I know how to sing or clap increasing and decreasing tempo. • I know how to order sounds to create a beginning, middle and an end. • I know how to create music in response to different starting points. • I know how to choose sounds which create an effect. • I know how to use symbols to represent sounds. • I know how to make connections between notations and musical sounds. • I know how to listen out for particular things when listening to music. • I know how to improve my own work.	• I know how to sing a tune with expression. • I know how to play clear notes on instruments. • I know how to use different elements in my composition. • I know how to create repeated patterns with different instruments. • I know how to compose melodies and songs. • I know how to create accompaniments for tunes. • I know how to combine different sounds to create a specific mood or feeling. • I know how to use musical words to describe a piece of music and compositions. • I know how to use musical words to describe what I like and do not like about a piece of music. • I know how to recognise the work of at least one famous composer. • I know how to improve my work; explaining how it has been improved.

A Year 4 musician	A Year 5 musician	A Year 6 musician
• I know how to perform a simple part rhythmically. • I know how to sing songs from memory with accurate pitch. • I know how to improvise using repeated patterns. • I know how to use notation to record and interpret sequences of pitches. • I know how to use notation to record compositions in a small group or on my own. • I know how to explain why silence is often needed in music and explain what effect it has. • I know how to identify the character in a piece of music. • I know how to identify and describe the different purposes of music. • I know how to begin to identify the style of work of Beethoven, Mozart and Elgar.	• I know how to breathe in the correct place when singing. • I know how to maintain my part whilst others are performing their part. • I know how to improvise within a group using melodic and rhythmic phrases. • I know how to change sounds or organise them differently to change the effect. • I know how to compose music which meets specific criteria. • I know how to use notation to record groups of pitches (chords). • I know how to use my music diary to record aspects of the composition process. • I know how to choose the most appropriate tempo for a piece of music. • I know how to describe, compare and evaluate music using musical vocabulary. • I know how to explain why I think music is successful or unsuccessful. • I know how to suggest improvement to my own work and that of others. • I know how to contrast the work of a famous composer with another, and explain my preferences.	• I know how to sing in harmony confidently and accurately. • I know how to perform parts from memory. • I know how to take the lead in a performance. • I know how to use a variety of different musical devices in my composition (including melody, rhythms and chords). • I know how to evaluate how the venue, occasion and purpose affects the way a piece of music is created. • I know how to analyse features within different pieces of music. • I know how to compare and contrast the impact that different composers from different times have had on people of that time.

Key Assessment Criteria Computing

A Year 1 computer user	A Year 2 computer user	A Year 3 computer user
Algorithms and programming • I create a series of instructions. • I plan a journey for a programmable toy. **Information technology** • I create digital content. • I store digital content. • I retrieve digital content. • I use a website. • I use a camera. • I record sound and play back. **Digital literacy** • I use technology safely. • I keep personal information private.	**Algorithms and programming** • I use a range of instructions (e.g. direction, angles, turns). • I test and amend a set of instructions. • I find errors and amend. (debug) • I write a simple program and test it. • I predict what the outcome of a simple program will be (logical reasoning). • I understand that algorithms are used on digital devices. • I understand that programs require precise instructions. **Information technology** • I organise digital content. • I retrieve and manipulate digital content. • I can navigate the web to complete simple searches. **Digital literacy** • I technology respectfully. • I know where to go for help if I am concerned. • I know how technology is used in school and outside of school.	**Algorithms and programming** • I design a sequence of instructions, including directional instructions. • I write programs that accomplish specific goals. • I work with various forms of input. • I work with various forms of output. **Information technology** • I use a range of software for similar purposes. • I collect information. • I design and create content. • I present information. • I search for information on the web in different ways. • I manipulate and improve digital images. **Digital literacy** • I use technology respectfully and responsibly. • I know different ways I can get help if I am concerned. • I understand what computer networks do and how they provide multiple services. • I discern where it is best to use technology and where it adds little or no value.

A Year 4 computer user	A Year 5 computer user	A Year 6 computer user
Algorithms and programming	**Algorithms and programming**	**Algorithms and programming**
• I experiment with variables to control models.	• I combine sequences of instructions and procedures to turn devices on and off.	• I design a solution by breaking a problem up.
• I give an on-screen robot specific instructions that takes them from A to B.	• I use technology to control an external device.	• I recognise that different solutions can exist for the same problem.
• I make an accurate prediction and explain why I believe something will happen (linked to programming).	• I design algorithms that use repetition & 2-way selection.	• I use logical reasoning to detect errors in algorithms.
• I de-bug a program.	**Information technology**	• I use selection in programs.
Information technology	• I analyse information.	• I work with variables.
• I select and use software to accomplish given goals.	• I evaluate information.	• I explain how an algorithm works.
• I collect and present data.	• I understand how search results are selected and ranked.	• I explore 'what if' questions by planning different scenarios for controlled devices.
• I produce and upload a podcast.	• I edit a film.	**Information technology**
Digital literacy	**Digital literacy**	• I select, use and combine software on a range of digital devices.
• I recognise acceptable and unacceptable behaviour using technology.	• I understand that you have to make choices when using technology and that not everything is true and/or safe.	• I use a range of technology for a specific project.
		Digital literacy
		• I discuss the risks of online use of technology.
		• I identify how to minimise risks.

A safe computer user in Year 1 and Year 2

Knowledge and understanding	Skills
• I understand the different methods of communication (e.g. email, online forums etc). • I know you should only open email from a known source. • I know the difference between email and communication systems such as blogs and wikis. • I know that websites sometimes include pop-ups that take me away from the main site. • I know that bookmarking is a way to find safe sites again quickly. • I have begun to evaluate websites and know that everything on the internet is not true. • I know that it is not always possible to copy some text and pictures from the internet. • I know that personal information should not be shared online. • I know I must tell a trusted adult immediately if anyone tries to meet me via the internet.	• I follow the school's safer internet rules. • I use the search engines agreed by the school. • I know what to do if I find something inappropriate online or something I am unsure of (including identifying people who can help; minimising screen; online reporting using school system etc.). • I use the internet for learning and communicating with others, making choices when navigating through sites. • I send and receive email as a class. • I recognise advertising on websites and learn to ignore it. • I use a password to access the secure network.

A safe computer user in Year 3 and Year 4

Knowledge and understanding

- I understand the need for rules to keep me safe when exchanging learning and ideas online.
- I recognise that information on the internet may not be accurate or reliable and may be used for bias, manipulation or persuasion.
- I understand that the internet contains fact, fiction and opinion and begin to distinguish between them.
- I use strategies to verify information, e.g. cross-checking.
- I understand the need for caution when using an internet search for images and what to do if I find an unsuitable image.
- I understand that copyright exists on most digital images, video and recorded music.
- I understand the need to keep personal information and passwords private.
- I understand that if I make personal information available online it may be seen and used by others.
- I know how to respond if asked for personal information or feel unsafe about content of a message.
- I recognise that cyber bullying is unacceptable and will be sanctioned in line with the school's policy.
- I know how to report an incident of cyber bullying.
- I know the difference between online communication tools used in school and those used at home.
- I understand the need to develop an alias for some public online use.
- I understand that the outcome of internet searches at home may be different than at school.

Skills

- I follow the school's safer internet rules.
- I recognise the difference between the work of others which has been copied (plagiarism) and re-structuring and re-presenting materials in ways which are unique and new.
- I identify when emails should not be opened and when an attachment may not be safe.
- I explain and demonstrate how to use email safely.
- I use different search engines.

A safe computer user in Year 5 and Year 6

Knowledge and understanding	Skills
• I discuss the positive and negative impact of the use of ICT in my own life, my friends and family. • I understand the potential risk of providing personal information online. • I recognise why people may publish content that is not accurate and understand the need to be critical evaluators of content. • I understand that some websites and/or pop-ups have commercial interests that may affect the way the information is presented. • I recognise the potential risks of using internet communication tools and understand how to minimise those risks (including scams and phishing). • I understand that some material on the internet is copyrighted and may not be copied or downloaded. • I understand that some messages may be malicious and know how to deal with this. • I understand that online environments have security settings, which can be altered, to protect the user. • I understand the benefits of developing a 'nickname' for online use. • I understand that some malicious adults may use various techniques to make contact and elicit personal information. • I know that it is unsafe to arrange to meet unknown people online. • I know how to report any suspicions. • I understand I should not publish other people's pictures or tag them on the internet without permission. • I know that content put online is extremely difficult to remove. • I know what to do if I discover something malicious or inappropriate.	• I follow the school's safer internet rules. • I make safe choices about the use of technology. • I use technology in ways which minimises risk. e.g. responsible use of online discussions, etc. • I create strong passwords and manage them so that they remain strong. • I independently, and with regard for e-safety, select and use appropriate communication tools to solve problems by collaborating and communicating with others within and beyond school. • I competently use the internet as a search tool. • I reference information sources. • I use appropriate strategies for finding, critically evaluating, validating and verifying information. e.g. using different keywords, skim reading to check relevance of information, cross checking with different websites or other non ICT resources. • I use knowledge of the meaning of different domain names and common website extensions (e.g. .co.uk; .com; .ac; .sch; .org; .gov; .net) to support validation of information.

Key Assessment Criteria
Design and Technology

A Year 1 designer	A Year 2 designer	A Year 3 designer
• I use my own ideas to make something.	• I think of an idea and plan what to do next.	• I prove that my design meets some set criteria.
• I describe how something works.	• I choose tools and materials and explain why I have chosen them.	• I follow a step-by-step plan, choosing the right equipment and materials.
• I cut food safely.		
• I make a product which moves.	• I join materials and components in different ways.	• I design a product and make sure that it looks attractive.
• I make my model stronger.	• I explain what went well with my work.	• I choose a material for both its suitability and its appearance.
• I explain to someone else how I want to make my product.	• I explain why I have chosen specific textiles.	• I select the most appropriate tools and techniques for a given task.
• I choose appropriate resources and tools.	• I measure materials to use in a model or structure.	• I make a product which uses both electrical and mechanical components.
• I make a simple plan before making.	• I describe the ingredients I am using.	• I work accurately to measure, make cuts and make holes.
		• I describe how food ingredients come together.

A Year 4 designer	A Year 5 designer	A Year 6 designer
• I use ideas from other people when I am designing.	• I come up with a range of ideas after collecting information from different sources.	• I use market research to inform my plans and ideas.
• I produce a plan and explain it.	• I produce a detailed, step-by-step plan.	• I follow and refine my plans.
• I evaluate and suggest improvements for my designs.	• I suggest alternative plans; outlining the positive features and draw backs.	• I justify my plans in a convincing way.
• I evaluate products for both their purpose and appearance.	• I explain how a product will appeal to a specific audience.	• I show that I consider culture and society in my plans and designs.
• I explain how I have improved my original design.	• I evaluate appearance and function against original criteria.	• I show that I can test and evaluate my products.
• I present a product in an interesting way.	• I use a range of tools and equipment competently.	• I explain how products should be stored and give reasons.
• I measure accurately.	• I make a prototype before make a final version.	• I work within a budget.
• I persevere and adapt my work when my original ideas do not work.	• I show that I can be both hygienic and safe in the kitchen.	• I evaluate my product against clear criteria.
• I know how to be both hygienic and safe when using food.		

Key Assessment Criteria

Physical Education

A Year 1 sports person	A Year 2 sports person	A Year 3 sports person
Games • I throw underarm. • I hit a ball with a bat. • I move and stop safely. • I throw and catch with both hands. • I throw and kick in different ways. **Gymnastics** • I make my body curled, tense, stretched and relaxed. • I control my body when travelling and balancing. • I copy sequences and repeat them. • I roll, curl, travel and balance in different ways. **Dance** • I move to music. • I copy dance moves. • I perform my own dance moves. • I make up a short dance. • I move safely in a space. **General** • I copy actions. • I repeat actions and skills. • I move with control and care. • I use equipment safely.	**Games** • I use hitting, kicking and/or rolling in a game. • I decide the best space to be in during a game. • I use a tactic in a game. • I follow rules. **Gymnastics** • I plan and perform a sequence of movements. • I improve my sequence based on feedback. • I think of more than one way to create a sequence which follows some 'rules'. • I work on my own and with a partner. **Dance** • I change rhythm, speed, level and direction in my dance. • I dance with control and coordination. • I make a sequence by linking sections together. • I use dance to show a mood or feeling. **General** • I copy and remember actions. • I talk about what is different from what I did and what someone else did.	**Games** • I throw and catch with control. • I am aware of space and use it to support team-mates and to cause problems for the opposition. • I know and use rules fairly. **Gymnastics** • I adapt sequences to suit different types of apparatus and criteria. • I explain how strength and suppleness affect performance. • I compare and contrast gymnastic sequences. **Dance** • I improvise freely and translate ideas from a stimulus into movement. • I share and create phrases with a partner and small group. • I repeat, remember and perform phrases. **Athletics** • I run at fast, medium and slow speeds; changing speed and direction. • I take part in a relay, remembering when to run and what to do. **Outdoor and adventurous** • I follow a map in a familiar context. • I use clues to follow a route. • I follow a route safely.

A Year 4 sports person	A Year 5 sports person	A Year 6 sports person
Games • I catch with one hand. • I throw and catch accurately. • I hit a ball accurately with control. • I keep possession of the ball. • I vary tactics and adapt skills depending on what is happening in a game.	**Games** • I gain possession by working a team. • I pass in different ways. • I use forehand and backhand with a racket. • I can field. • I choose a tactic for defending and attacking. • I use a number of techniques to pass, dribble and shoot.	**Games** • I play to agreed rules. • I explain rules to others. • I can umpire. • I make a team and communicate a plan. • I lead others in a game situation.
Gymnastics • I work in a controlled way. • I include change of speed and direction. • I include a range of shapes. • I work with a partner to create, repeat and improve a sequence with at least three phases.	**Gymnastics** • I make complex extended sequences. • I combine action, balance and shape. • I perform consistently to different audiences.	**Gymnastics** • I combine my own work with that of others. • I sequences to specific timings.
Dance • I take the lead when working with a partner or group. • I use dance to communicate an idea.	**Dance** • I compose my own dances in a creative way. • I perform to an accompaniment. • My dance shows clarity, fluency, accuracy and consistency.	**Dance** • I develop sequences in a specific style. • I choose my own music and style.
Athletics • I run over a long distance. • I sprint over a short distance. • I throw in different ways. • I hit a target. • I jump in different ways.	**Athletics** • I controlled when taking off and landing. • I throw with accuracy. • I combine running and jumping.	**Athletics** • I demonstrate stamina.
Outdoor and adventurous • I follow a map in a (more demanding) familiar context. • I follow a route within a time limit.	**Outdoor and adventurous** • I follow a map into an unknown location. • I use clues and a compass to navigate a route. • I change my route to overcome a problem. • I use new information to change my route.	**Outdoor and adventurous** • I plan a route and a series of clues for someone else. • I plan with others, taking account of safety and danger.

Key Assessment Criteria
Foreign Language

A Year 1/2 international speaker	A Year 3/4 international speaker	A Year 5/6 international speaker
Non Statutory		
Spoken language • I join in with songs and rhymes. • I respond to a simple command. • I answer with a single word. • I answer with a short phrase. • I ask an appropriate question. • I name people. • I name places. • I name objects. • I use set phrases. • I choose the right word to complete a phrase. • I choose the right word to complete a short sentence. Reading • I read and understand single words. • I read and understand short phrases. • I use simple dictionaries to find the meaning of words. Writing • I write single words correctly. • I label a picture. • I copy a simple word or phrase.	Spoken language • I name and describe people. • I name and describe a place. • I name and describe an object. • I have a short conversation saying 3-4 things. • I give a response using a short phrase. • I am starting to speak in sentences. Reading • I read and understand a short passage using familiar language. • I explain the main points in a short passage. • I read a passage independently. • I use a bilingual dictionary or glossary to look up new words. Writing • I write phrases from memory. • I write 2-3 short sentences on a familiar topic. • I say what I like/dislike about a familiar topic.	Spoken language • I hold a simple conversation with at least 4 exchanges. • I use my knowledge of grammar to speak correctly. Reading • I understand a short story or factual text and note the main points. • I use the context to work out unfamiliar words. Writing • I write a paragraph of 4-5 sentences. • I substitute words and phrases.